THE POETIC SCRIPTURES OF LUKE

THE POETIC SCRIPTURES OF LUKE

GOD'S WORD IN RHYTHM & RHYME

MICHAEL D. WESTER

Printed in the United States of America
ISBN 978-1-64133-628-4 (sc)
ISBN 978-1-64133-629-1 (hc)
ISBN 978-1-64133-630-7 (e)

Library of Congress Control Number: 2019917231

Artwork and Cover Design by ***Cameron Klingenberg***

Inspirational / Worship and Devotion / Non-Fiction
19.11.15

Lighthouse Publication
1553 E. Caro Road
Caro, MI 48723

www.lighthousepublication.com

CONTENTS

INTRODUCTION

This is the second book of the *Poetic Scriptures*, putting God's Word to rhythm and rhyme. After working on the writings of the apostle John, I was encouraged to work on more of the Scriptures. The Scriptures of Luke, although encompassing only two writings, comprise the biggest portion of the New Testament by any one author. The task was long and hard but very rewarding. I thank my wife, Donna, for her support in this endeavor.

Before presenting the book for publishing, the work was submitted to those knowledgeable in the Scriptures for review to make sure it accurately reflected the original language in which Luke wrote. As in the case of the previous work, occasionally I elaborated on the text. I may have elaborated on a meaning of a word. I may have derived information from another verse to complete an idea. Whenever a major elaboration was done, I noted it by using an asterisk (*). If any extra explanation was needed, I referenced it as an endnote.

Having the Scriptures in rhyme has many applications. I have already put it to use in several ways, such as family devotions, in sermons, at funerals, and even as a drama. One time our church put on the Christmas story using the poetic narrative in Luke. We had various people act out the parts and even had them speak their parts. It was exciting to see how rhythm and rhyme captured the attention of the audience.

My prayer has always been that every person can come face to face with God's Word so as to reflect, meditate, and apply. God's Word is not something just to put in our minds but to plant in our hearts so that we truly bring Him glory in all that we say or do. Perhaps a collection of the Scriptures in rhythm and rhyme will be a tool to that end.

I pray that all will be blessed by this unique way in presenting the Scriptures. I pray that the *Poetic Scriptures* will not just affect the mind but also infect the heart with God's Word.

THE POETIC GOSPEL OF LUKE

1:1 Many people have attempted
To both research and record
Certain events that did occur
In connection with the Lord.[1]

1:2 Those who were with Him from the start,
Testimony they did convey
As eyewitnesses and servants
To the word we have today.

1:3 And so it seemed appropriate
That I write this down for you,
Most excellent Theophilus,
In an orderly review.

For I've examined everything
From the beginning with care,
Writing down chronologically
Events of which you're aware.

1:4 Although you have been taught the truth,
I write this that you may know
The exact facts of what you've heard
In the order that they go.

1:5 When King Herod of Judea
Was ruling the Judean land,
A man named Zacharias came,
And as a priest he did stand.

The division of Abijah,
Was his priestly claim.*
From Aaron's daughters was his wife.
Elizabeth was her name.

1:6 They both obeyed all God's commands.
They were righteous in His sight.
They obeyed the Lord's requirements.
Without blame they practiced right.

1:7 Now Elizabeth was barren.
They had no daughter or son,
And both of them were past the years
Of ever producing one.

1:8 When Zacharias's division
Was in the temple one week,
He served as priest before the Lord,
But this work he could not seek.*

1:9 For the custom of the priesthood
Was to determine by lot
Who would burn incense to the Lord,
And this one-time choice[2] he got.

1:10 He was in the sanctuary
As the people outside prayed,
While burning incense to the Lord,
Which on the altar he laid.*

1:11 An angel of the Lord appeared
(To Zacharias's fright),
Standing by the altar of incense,
Specifically on the right.

1:12 Who it was that appeared to him
He was wholly unaware;*
He was troubled and filled with fear
When he saw the angel there.

1:13 "Zacharias, don't be afraid,"
Said the angel to calm his fears,
"For your petitions have been heard;
They have reached God's very ears.*

"Elizabeth is not barren.*
Your wife will bear you a boy,
And John is the name you'll give him.
1:14 He'll give you gladness and joy.

1:15 "Many will rejoice at his birth,
For great he'll be in God's sight.
He must not drink wine or liquor,
Living as a Nazarite.[3]

"With the Holy Spirit of God,
He will certainly be filled
While in the womb of his mother,
For this the Lord God has willed.*

1:16 “Many of the sons of Israel
To their Lord God he will turn.
1:17 He will go ahead of the Lord
With both focus and concern.*

“He will turn the hearts of fathers
Back to their daughters and sons.
He’ll turn the disobedient
To the way of righteous ones.

“In Elijah’s spirit and might,
The people he will prepare
For the arrival of the Lord,
So of Him they’ll be aware.”*

1:18 Zacharias then did address
The angel about this word,
“How will I be certain of this
Since to me this sounds absurd?*

“Since I am very old indeed,
Since I’m well advanced in years,
And since my wife is very old,
Quite absurd your news appears.”*

1:19 The angel answered with these words,
“Gabriel, that is my name,
Who stands before God, sent to you
With this good news to proclaim.

“I have spoken these words to you,
For you to gladly receive.*
1:20 You will not be able to speak
Because you did not believe.

"You will not be able to speak
Until the day this takes place.
All this will happen in due time
In accordance with God's grace."*

1:21 The crowd waiting for Zacharias
Wondered about the delay,
Why the priest was still inside
The sanctuary that day.

1:22 When Zacharias came outside,
He could not speak with his voice.
To communicate by signing
Was his one and only choice.*

The crowd had realized from his signs
Just what all of this did mean,
That inside the sanctuary
Was a vision he had seen.

1:23 To serve as priest he continued
Just as it was intended.*
Then he returned back to his home
After his service ended.

1:24 His wife, Elizabeth, conceived
At the time God's plan was due.[4]
For five whole months she hid herself,
Hiding from the public view.

1:25 "The Lord has dealt with me this way,"
Elizabeth did exclaim,
"Looking on me with grace these days,
Removing from man my shame!"

1:26 In her sixth month of pregnancy,
Gabriel, the messenger,
Was sent by God to a virgin
To give the good news to her.*

This virgin lived in Nazareth,
A city in Galilee,
1:27 Engaged to a man named Joseph
Of Davidic ancestry.

Now the virgin's name was Mary,
1:28 And Gabriel entered her place.
"Hail," he said. "The Lord is with you,
You who are filled up with grace!"

1:29 But Mary was greatly troubled
By the statement of this word,
Wondering what kind of greeting
It was that she just had heard.

1:30 So the angel said this to her:
"Mary, stop all of your fear!
For you have found favor with God,
1:31 And His grace you now must hear.[5]

"You will conceive within your womb
And will give birth to a son,
And you must call His name Jesus,
For He is the Promised One.*

1:32 "He will be great, and by this name,
'The Most High's Son' He'll be known,
And the Lord God will give to Him
His ancestor David's throne.

1:33 "And over the house of Jacob
He will reign eternally,
And His kingdom will continue,
For its end will never be."

1:34 Then to the angel Mary said,
"Just how can this thing occur?
For I do not know any man,
And I am a virgin, sir."

1:35 "The Holy Spirit will do this,"
The angel gave his reply.
"And there will overshadow you
The power of the Most High.

"For this reason the holy Child,
Who out of your womb will come,
Because He's not from any man,*
He will be called God's Son.

1:36 "Look! Your cousin Elizabeth
In her old age has conceived.
She who was considered barren,
A son she has now received.

"And she is now six months along
In the course of her pregnancy.
1:37 Nothing will be too hard for God.
That's what I want you to see."*

1:38 Then Mary replied, "Look on me!
As the Lord's slave I accept!
Let it be done as you have said."
Then from her the angel left.

1:39 At this time Mary got ready,
And then left her place with haste.
Eager to see Elizabeth,
There was not any time to waste.*

She went into the hill country
To this one Judean town
1:40 And entered Zacharias's house,
Where Elizabeth she found.

1:41 As soon as Mary greeted her,
The baby leaped up inside,
And filled with the Holy Spirit,
1:42 Elizabeth loudly cried,

"Among all women you are blessed,
And blessed is the Child you'll bear.
1:43 How is it that my Lord's mother
Should come before me and share?

1:44 "For even before seeing you,
As soon as I heard your voice,
The baby that is in my womb,
He leaped up and did rejoice.

1:45 "So blessed is she who did believe,
For surely it will occur,
Everything that had been spoken
By the Lord unto her."

1:46 Mary said, "Honor to the Lord
Is my own soul's behavior,
1:47 And my spirit has found great joy
In God who is my Savior.

1:48 "For His bond slave's lowly status
He had consideration.
From now on I'll be called blessed
By every generation.

1:49 "For the mighty powerful One,
(His power I do proclaim),*
Has accomplished great things for me.
Also holy is His name.

1:50 "His mercy does extend to all
Who give Him admiration.
His mercy does extend to them
In every generation.

1:51 "With His arm He has done great deeds.
Proud hearts He's caused to crumble,
1:52 Bringing rulers down from their thrones,
And lifting high the humble.

1:53 "He has satisfied the hungry
With such good things to possess,
Yet He has sent away the rich
With nothing but emptiness.

1:54 "Israel His servant He has helped,
Recalling His mercy indeed,
1:55 The eternal word to our fathers,
To Abraham and his seed."

1:56 Mary stayed with Elizabeth
For a time *(let it be known),
A time that spanned about three months
Before returning back home.

1:57 Now the moment of fulfillment
For Elizabeth did come
To bring forth whom was in her womb,
And she gave birth to a son.

1:58 Her neighbors and her relatives
Came to hear of the Lord's choice,
Of showing great mercy to her.
So with her they did rejoice.

1:59 The eighth day following the birth
They arrived to circumcise,
And give a name to the baby.
"Zacharias," were their cries.

They wished to give the father's name
Because this was often done,*
1:60 But Elizabeth objected,
"John is the name of my son."

1:61 They said to her, "Why call him John?
No relative has that name!"
1:62 So they motioned to his father
As to what name he would claim.

1:63 He asked for a writing tablet
So his choice he could present.
"His name is John," is what he wrote,
Which brought great astonishment.

1:64 Right then his mouth just opened up,
For his tongue had been set free.
He was speaking praises to God,
1:65 And wonder spread rapidly.

Yes, all those living around them
Were filled with wonder and awe.
The whole Judean hill country,
Their attention this did draw.

1:66 They'd discuss the events and ask,
"Just who will this child become?"
They knew that the hand of the Lord
Was surely upon this one.

1:67 Now his father, Zacharias,
When his tongue had been set free,[6]
Was filled with the Holy Spirit
As he spoke this prophecy:

1:68 "Praise the Lord God of Israel!
For to us with help He's come,
And effected for His people
His redemption through this one.

1:69 "In His servant David's house
For us He has lifted out
A mighty horn of salvation
1:70 Which His prophets spoke about.

1:71 "Salvation from our enemies,
From all those who hate us so,
Through the mouths of holy prophets
He prophesied long ago.

1:72 "To show mercy to our fathers,
To remember what He said
As to His holy covenant
That He made with one now dead.[7]

1:73 "This oath He made with Abraham,
Our forefather whom He chose,
1:74 He granted to us, saving us
Out of the hand of our foes.

"Yes, He granted this oath to us
So to serve Him without fears
1:75 In holiness and righteousness
Throughout all our days and years.

1:76 "'The prophet of the Most High God,'
My child, of you He will say,[8]
For you will go before the Lord
To prepare for Him the way.

1:77 "For the knowledge of salvation
With God's people you will share
Through the forgiveness of their sins
1:78 Due to our God's tender care.

“By His mercy to us will come
The rising that’s from on high
1:79 To shine on those sitting in darkness
And on those about to die.

“The rising from on high will come
To make all the darkness cease*
To guide our feet so we can walk
Into the pathway of peace.”

1:80 The child was growing in stature,
In spiritual strength as well.
He lived in deserts ’til the time
He appeared to Israel.

2:1 In those days Caesar Augustus
Sent to the Roman nation[9]
A decree that all be registered,
The entire population.

2:2 This was the first census taken
Of the whole population
While Quirinius ruled Syria
That required registration.*

2:3 And everyone was traveling
According to the decree*
To register for the census
In the town of his family.

2:4 Joseph went up from Nazareth,
A city in Galilee,
Into the Judean region,
To the town of his family.

This town, which is called Bethlehem,
Was the town of David, *the king.
Since Joseph was from David's line,
To there he was traveling.

2:5 He traveled along with Mary
For their names to be compiled.
Now Mary was engaged to him
And was expecting a child.

2:6 While they were there in Bethlehem,
The day did finally come
For Mary to deliver her Child,
2:7 And she gave birth to a son.

This Son was Mary's firstborn child.
She wrapped Him in swaddling clothes.
Since there was no room in the inn,
A manger for Him she chose.

2:8 There were shepherds in that region
Out in the pastures at night,
Watching over their flock of sheep
2:9 When suddenly shined a light.

Standing before their very eyes,
The Lord's angel did appear.
The Lord's glory shined around them,
And they all were filled with fear.

2:10 The angel said, "Don't be afraid,
For listen to what I bring:
Good news about a joy that's great,
Good news about this one King.[10]

"The good news which I bring to you,
To all people it will extend.
So stop being so terrified,
But listen and comprehend.*

2:11 "Today in the town of David
There is one to be adored,*
A savior who's been born for you,
The Savior, who's Christ the Lord.

2:12 "Now this will be the sign for you,
You will find Him in this way:
You'll find a babe in swaddling clothes,
Lying in a bin of hay."

2:13 And suddenly with the angel
A great multitude appeared,
A heavenly army praising God,
Exclaiming as they all cheered.*

2:14 "Glory and peace!" they did exclaim,
"The glory pertains to God,
He who's in the highest places.
All His work we do applaud.*

"Glory and peace!" they did exclaim,
"For this peace God does instill[11]
To people living on the earth,
Those described by His goodwill."

2:15 Into heaven the angels went,
Away from the shepherds' sight.
To each other the shepherds said,
"Let us go this very night.

"Let's go right now to Bethlehem.
Let us see this great event
Which the Lord has made know to us."
2:16 And quickly the shepherds went.

Mary and Joseph they soon found.
The Baby they found as well.
When they saw Him in the manger,
2:17 The news they began to tell.

Everything that was told to them,
All the angel said that night,*
All the things about this Child,
To them all, they did recite.

2:18 And as the shepherds' words were heard,
Great wonder they did impart,
2:19 But Mary treasured all their words,
Pondering them in her heart.

2:20 The shepherds returned praising God
For all that they saw and heard.
They glorified God who fulfilled
All of the angel's word.[12]

2:21 Now when the Child was circumcised,
The name Jesus He received
As the angel had commanded
Before He had been conceived.

As was the custom this occurred,
The naming, *that is to say,[13]
The same time He was circumcised,
Taking place on the eighth day.

2:22 And then they waited to complete
Their days of purification,
Stated in the Law of Moses
Before the dedication.

They went up to Jerusalem
To present Him to the Lord
And then to sacrifice two doves
Which was all they could afford.[14]

2:23 As is written in the Lord's Law
About the dedication:
"Each firstborn male must be to God[15]
A holy presentation."

2:24 As is written in the Lord's Law
Concerning the sacrifice:
"Two young pigeons or else two doves
For the poor, these will suffice."[16]

2:25 Now take note of a certain man
Who was present when they came.
This man was righteous and devout.
Simeon was this man's name.

He was eagerly waiting for
Israel's Consolation.
The Holy Spirit upon him
2:26 Gave him a revelation.

The Holy Spirit promised him
That before death would arise
The Lord's Christ, the Anointed One,[17]
He would see with his own eyes.

2:27 He had come into the temple,
Guided by the Spirit's will
As the parents brought in Jesus,
The Law's custom to fulfill.

2:28 He took the Child into his arms
As praises to God he gave:
2:29 "Now Lord, You have fulfilled Your word
Unto me Your faithful slave.

"You can let me depart in peace
2:30 Because my own eyes did find
Your salvation, which You've prepared
2:31 In the presence of mankind.

2:32 "He's a light of revelation
To the nations of the earth.
Salvation You've prepared for them*
By virtue of this One's birth.*

"And to Your people Israel,
He is a glorious light.
Salvation You've prepared for them*
As the prophets did recite."*

2:33 Now the Child's father and mother
Were deeply impressed, amazed,
At what they heard about their Son,
Which Simeon had just phrased.

2:34 Then Simeon blessed His parents
With some words to their delight,
But to the Child's mother, Mary,
This message he did recite:

"Take special note about this Child,
For this He has been assigned:
Many in Israel will rise up,
And their Savior they will find.*

"Others will stumble in Israel.
To Him their hearts will be closed.*
As a sign He has been destined
To constantly be opposed.

2:35 "This is so that thoughts from the hearts
Of many will be made known,
And as for you, a sword will pierce
The very soul that you own."

2:36 Now a prophetess was there too,
The daughter of Phanuel,
Hannah from the tribe of Asher,
Of the tribes of Israel.[18]

Hannah was well advanced in age.
Of this we do not know more:[19]
She was married seven years,
2:37 Then was widowed eighty-four.

Hannah never left the temple,
But she served there night and day.
Fasting and praying marked her life
As in the temple she'd stay.

2:38 As Simeon finished his words,
Hannah came up, standing by,
And began giving thanks to God.
The thanksgivings she did cry.

Since Jerusalem's redemption
So many were awaiting,
Words concerning this little Child
To these she was relating.

2:39 After performing everything
As far as the Law[20] was concerned,
To their own town in Galilee,
To Nazareth, they returned.

2:40 The Child was growing in stature,
And becoming very strong.
He grew in wisdom as God's grace
Was upon Him all along.

2:41 Now during the Passover feast
It was Jesus's parents' trend
To go up to Jerusalem.
Every year they would attend.

2:42 The year the Boy became age twelve,
To Jerusalem they went
To celebrate the Jewish feast,
Their custom for this event.

2:43 After observing all the days
That Levitical law defined,[21]
The parents were returning home,
But had left Jesus behind.

The Boy stayed in Jerusalem,
His parents being unaware.
2:44 They assumed He was among them
In the caravan somewhere.

After traveling one full day
When Jesus they could not find
Among their friends or relatives,
2:45 They knew they'd left Him behind.

They went back to Jerusalem,
And searched for Him everywhere.
2:46 After three days of being gone,
They found Him in no despair.*

He was sitting in the temple
Among teachers of the Law,[22]
Listening to and questioning them,
2:47 Putting the people in awe.

For all who heard Him were amazed
At all His understanding,
At His answers to the questions
That teachers were demanding.*

2:48 Even when His parents saw Him,
Also them He did amaze.
His mother then went up to Him,
And this question she did raise.

"Why, Child, have You done this to us?
You must take a careful view.[23]
Your father and I were anxious
As we were searching for You."

2:49 He answered them with a question,
"Why were you searching for Me?
Don't you know that My Father's things[24]
Are what My focus must be?"

2:50 This statement that He spoke to them,
They both did not understand;
2:51 However, He still left with them,
Submitting to their command.*

They traveled down to Nazareth
To the town in which they stayed.*
And His parents' authority
He respected and obeyed.

And Mary treasured in her heart
Everything that happened there.
Jesus kept submitting to them,
Being in His parents' care.*

2:52 Jesus kept growing in stature
As wisdom from Him did swell.
He was finding favor with God
And with people as well.

3:1 Now sometime in the fifteenth year
Of Tiberius Caesar's reign,
To the son of Zacharias
The message of God then came.

Pontius Pilate also governed
Judea in that same year.
As for the region Galilee,
Herod was a tetrarch here.

Philip was tetrarch over these:
(Philip was Herod's brother)
Ituraea was one region,
Trachonitis, the other.

And Lysanias was tetrarch.
Abilene was his domain.
3:2 Annas and also Caiaphas
As high priests these two did reign.

Now the son of Zacharias,
Or John as was this man's name,
Was living in the wilderness
When to him God's message came.

3:3 John went into all the districts
Around the Jordan River.
In response to the word of God,*
This word he did deliver:

Forgiveness of sins is given
For each one who would consent
To a baptism confessing
That from sins they do repent.

3:4 As Isaiah the prophet says,
That some person[25] did record,
"In the desert the voice will cry,
'Prepare the way for the Lord!

"'Make straight the paths that He travels.
3:5 Every valley will be filled.
All high spots will be leveled,
Every mountain and each hill.

"'Crooked roadways will be straightened.
The rough roads will be smoothed out,
3:6 And God's salvation will be seen
By mankind from all about.'"

3:7 Now John was saying to the crowds
Who for baptism did come,
"You offspring of snakes, who warned you
From the coming wrath to run?

3:8 "You must produce the kind of fruit
That shows you truly repent.
Don't say, 'Our father is Abraham.'
With this do not be content.*

"I tell you God is capable.
Yes, God most certainly can.*
He can raise up from these stones
Descendants for Abraham.

3:9 "The ax even now has been placed
To strike the tree's very root,
And so each tree is cut down and burned
That does not produce good fruit."

3:10 "What must we do?" the crowd would ask.
Then to them John would declare,
3:11 By giving them some examples
Of the kind of fruit to bear.*

"Let the one who has two tunics
Share with the one who has none,
And let the one who possesses food
Do likewise, *and do not shun."

3:12 Some tax collectors came to John,
"Teacher, what must we do?
Since we're coming for baptism,*
What is required by you?"

3:13 He replied to them with this word,
"Taxes for Rome you transact.*
You have been ordered what to take.
Take no more than what's exact."

3:14 Some soldiers also came to John.
They also from him did ask,
"And what will you require from us?
What manner should be our task?"

"Take from no one money by force,"
John to the soldiers did say.
"Don't falsely accuse anyone,
And be content with your pay."

3:15 The crowd was reasoning in their hearts
In a very expectant state,
Wondering if John was the Christ,
3:16 But these thoughts he did negate.*

John answered them and said to all,
"There comes One greater than I,
And the straps upon His sandals
I'm not worthy to untie.

"I, John, baptize you in water
According to your desire,*
But in these He will baptize you:
The Holy Spirit and fire.

3:17 "And in His hand He holds His fork
To clear out His threshing floor.
The chaff He'll burn with undying fire.
The wheat in His barn He'll store."

3:18 So John was preaching the good news
To the people in this way.
And with many other urgings,
The gospel he did relay.

3:19 John rebuked the tetrarch Herod,
For a wife he did acquire,[26]
His brother's wife Herodias,
To please his own desire.*

John rebuked him for much evil,
For in much things he did fail.
3:20 Then Herod added more evil
By locking up John in jail.

3:21 Now as the masses were baptized,
Jesus was baptized too.
As He was engaged in prayer,
Heaven opened up in view.

3:22 The Holy Spirit did descend
Akin to that of a dove,
Visibly lighting on Jesus,
Coming from heaven above.

Then a voice did speak from heaven.
From Scripture it did recite,[27]
"You are My Son, My beloved One.
In You I obtain delight."

3:23 Jesus began to minister
At about thirty years old.
Assumed to be Joseph's son,
His true lineage must be told.[28]

Now all the true progenitors
Will be listed one by one.
In every case Jesus is
That progenitor's son.[29]

Now the first male progenitor
Is His grandfather, Eli.
3:24 Jesus is the son of that man,
Of Matthat, and of Levi.

Jesus is the son of Melchi.
This name is a common one.
Melchi in Hebrew means *my king*,
And Jesus is Jannai's son.

Jesus is the son of Joseph,
Whose name is by no means odd.
3:25 He's the son of Mattathias,
Whose name means *a gift from God.*

Jesus is the son of Amos,
Whose name means *a weight to bear.*
Jesus is the son of Nahum,
Whose name means *comfort* or *care.*

He's son of Hesli and Naggai.
3:26 Also Jesus is Maath's son.
He's the son of Mattathias
(different than the other one).

He's son of Semein, whose name means
Hearers of the word I had.
Jesus is the son of Josech,
Translated as *God does add.*

He's son of Joda, whose name means
God will be praised and awed.
3:27 He is the son of Joanan,
Translated as *grace of God.*

Jesus is the son of Rhesa,
Whose name means *chief* or *head.*
He's the son of Zerubbabel.
The captives' return he led.[30]

He's of Shealtiel, Neri, Melchi.
3:28 (Recall Melchi means *my king.*)
He's of Addi and of Cosam,
And that name means *divining.*

He is the son of Elmadam,
Translated as *measurement.*
And Jesus is the son of Er,
Translated as *vigilant.*

3:29 Jesus is the son of Jesus,
(Greek spelling, I don't abort).[31]
He's the son of Eliezer,
Meaning *God is his support.*

Jesus is the son of Jorim,
Translated as *lift up high.*
Jesus is the son of Matthat,
And He's the son of Levi.

3:30 He's of Simeon and Judah.
Both come from the Hebrew race.
He's of Joseph and of Jonam,
Translated as *God gives grace.*

He's the son of Eliakim.
3:31 Son of Melea is He,
Son of Menna and Mattatha
And Nathan in Chronicles 3.[32]

Jesus is the son of David,
A sheep herder in his youth,[33]
3:32 Son of Jesse, Obed, Boaz,
The one who did marry Ruth.[34]

Jesus is the son of Salmon,
(or Sala as the Greek spells).[35]
Jesus is the son of Nahshon,
Whose name means *he who foretells.*

3:33 He's the son of Amminadab.
He's of Admin and of Ram,
Of Hezron, Perez, Judah, Jacob,
3:34 Of Isaac and Abraham.

He's son of Terah, of Nahor,
3:35 Son of Serug and of Reu,
Son of Peleg and of Heber,
And the son of Shelah too.

3:36 Jesus is the son of Cainan.
He's the son of Arphaxad.
He's son of Shem and of Noah.
(Noah built the ark for God.)[36]

3:37 He's of Lamech, of Methuselah,
He who lived the longest days.[37]
Jesus is the son of Enoch,
Whom God to heaven did raise.[38]

Jesus is the son of Jared.
He's son of Mahalaleel.
Jesus is also of Cainan,
Or Kenan, as Hebrews spell. [39]

3:38 He's son of Enosh and of Seth.
(Both lived when God's name was awed.)[40]
Jesus is the son of Adam.
Jesus is the Son of God.

4:1 And filled with the Holy Spirit,
From the Jordan Jesus went.
Following the Spirit's leading,
In the desert He was sent.

4:2 For forty days He wandered there.
As for food, He did not eat.
He was also being tempted
By the Devil He did meet.

After fasting for forty days,
Hunger He began to feel,[41]
Hunger pains within His stomach.*
He was ready for a meal.*

4:3 But the Devil tempted Jesus,
"Now command this stone," he said,
"For since You are the Son of God,
Make the stone become Your bread."

4:4 But Jesus answered back to him
Without speaking to the stone,*
"It is written that man must not
Live life upon bread alone."

4:5 The Devil led Him way up high.[42]
For Jesus he did design
A glimpse of all the earth's kingdoms
In just one moment of time.

4:6 Then the Devil said to Jesus,
"I'll give You all their power,
Also all their glory with it.
All this on You I'll shower.*

"For all this has been given me
To give to the one I choose.
4:7 So if You would just worship me,
This gift I will not refuse."

4:8 But Jesus answered back to him,
"What is written I observe,
'You must worship the Lord your God.
Only Him you are to serve.'"

4:9 He led Him to Jerusalem,
And there he had Jesus stand
Upon the temple's highest point.
To Him he gave a command.

"Because You are the Son of God,
Throw Yourself down from up here,
4:10 For in the Scriptures that You know
A promise for You is clear.*

"'He'll give His angels the command
To guard You when You are thrown,
4:11 And on their hands they'll hold You up
So Your foot strikes not a stone.'"

4:12 Jesus answered, saying to him,
"This command the Lord[43] has stressed,
'You must not try the Lord your God.
No, Him you must never test.'"

4:13 And when the Devil did complete
Every single tempting line,
He went away from His presence
Until an opportune time.

4:14 In the power of the Spirit
Jesus proceeded to head
To the region of Galilee,
Where the news of Him did spread.

News did spread throughout the district.
4:15 At Jesus all were amazed[44]
As He taught in their synagogues.
By everyone He was praised.

4:16 It was the practice of Jesus
On every Sabbath day
To enter in the synagogue.
It was His usual way.*

When Jesus came to Nazareth,
The town in which He was reared,
One Sabbath in the synagogue
He publicly appeared.*

He stood up to read the Scriptures.
4:17 In His hands was placed a scroll.
It was the prophet Isaiah.
These writings He did unroll.

He unrolled the scroll to this place
Because He was appointed:[45]
4:18 "The Lord's Spirit is upon Me
Since Me He has anointed.

"He has anointed Me to preach
The gospel news to the poor,
To proclaim release to captives,
And their freedom to restore.

"He has sent Me out to proclaim
To those unable to see
That their sight will be recovered,
From blindness to be set free.

"He has sent Me out to proclaim
Freedom to all the oppressed,
4:19 And the year of the Lord's favor
He has sent Me to attest."

4:20 He rolled up the scroll, gave it back
To the helper that was there.
He then sat down before them all
As all eyes at Him did stare.

Everyone in the synagogue
Was wondering what He might say.[46]
4:21 He said to them, "In your hearing,
This Scripture comes true today."

4:22 Now all were speaking well of Him.
With amazement they were filled.
They wondered at these gracious words
Which out of His mouth had spilled.

They were saying to one another,
"Is this man not Joseph's son?"
4:23 Then Jesus said to all of them
Whose approval He had won:*

"There is no doubt that you will quote
This parable to My face:
'Physician, take your medicine.
Bring healing to your own case.[47]

"'All You did in Capernaum,
Which our own ears have received,
Do also here in Your own town
That your works may be believed.'"*

4:24 Then to all the people He spoke
A parable that He phrased,
"Truly no prophet is welcome
In the town which he was raised.

4:25 "For truly throughout Israel
Many widows did reside
During the days of Elijah
When the sky did not provide.

"A span of three years and six months
Heaven gave no rain at all,
And over the entire land
A great famine did befall.

4:26 "And yet Elijah was not sent
To a widow living there,
But to the one of Zarephath,
In Sidon, that is where.

4:27 "And in the time of Elisha,
The next prophet *of the Lord,
Many lepers in Israel
Had great need to be restored.

"Yet not one leper in the land
Became cleansed *by the Lord's word
Except Naaman, the Syrian.
Just his leprosy was cured."

4:28 Then all those in the synagogue
Reacted to what they heard.
They all were filled with intense rage
Upon hearing Jesus's word.

4:29 They all got up and threw Him out,
Forcing Him out of the town
Which had been built upon a hill
Where they wished to throw Him down.

Coming to the brow of the hill,
To kill Him was their intent.*
4:30 But Jesus passed through all of them,
And on His journey He went.

4:31 He went down to Capernaum,
A city in Galilee.
On each Sabbath He was teaching
4:32 With immense authority.

And all the people were amazed
At the message that He brought
Since a certain[48] authority
Accompanied what He taught.

4:33 A man was in the synagogue,
But within him did reside
An unclean, demonic spirit,
And in a loud voice he cried:

4:34 "Ha! O Jesus of Nazareth,
Commonality we have none.
Have You come here to destroy us?
I know You're God's Holy One!"

4:35 "Be quiet," Jesus ordered him.
"Exit out!" He did assert.
As the demon threw the man down,
He came out but caused no hurt.

4:36 Amazement came on all of them.
With one another they conferred.
They were saying to one another,
"Of what sort is this One's word?

"In authority and power,
unclean spirits He commands,
And they respond by coming out
According to His demands."*

4:37 And this report concerning Him
Was being spread all around.
Into all surrounding places
Testimony did resound.

4:38 After leaving the synagogue,
Jesus entered Simon's house.
In his home there was this lady,
The mother of Simon's spouse.

She had been struck with a fever,
One that was very severe.
They asked Jesus on her behalf.
4:39 So to her He did draw near.*

Now Jesus stood right over her,
Telling the fever to fall.
The fever left. She got right up
And ministered to them all.

4:40 And as the sun was going down,
All those who had someone ill
Brought them to Jesus with the hope
Their healing He would fulfill.*

There were all kinds of diseases
Represented in this field.
On each one Jesus laid His hands,
And each one of them was healed.

4:41 Demons also were coming out
Of the many people there.
"You are the Son of God," they'd shout.
Of the Christ they were aware.

Since they knew Him to be the Christ,
Their cries He would reprimand.
He would not permit them to speak,
And they obeyed His command.*

4:42 When the next day finally dawned,
The crowd He then did leave.
He traveled to a lonely place,
Isolation to achieve.

The crowd began searching for Him,
And Him they finally found.
They tried to keep Him from leaving,
Wanting to keep Him around.

4:43 Jesus told them, "To this I'm bound.
Other cities I must reach.
I must proclaim good news to them.
Of God's kingdom I must preach.

"For that is the reason I was sent.
Others I must be reaching."
4:44 In the Judean synagogues
Jesus continued preaching.

5:1 One day by Lake Gennesaret
As Jesus was standing near,
The crowd began to press on Him
For the word of God to hear.

5:2 He saw at the edge of the lake
Two empty boats sitting there.
The fishermen who had left them
Were washing their nets with care.

5:3 Jesus stepped into Simon's boat
(The Simon mentioned before).[49]
He asked Simon to push it out
A short distance from the shore.

Then He sat down inside the boat.
The crowd He began to teach,
5:4 And then He instructed Simon
After completing His speech:

"Push the boat even farther out
Into the water that's deep.
Then lower all your fishing nets
So that a catch you may reap."

5:5 Simon replied, "We've toiled all night,
But no snagging has occurred,
But Master I'll let down the nets
In accordance to Your word."

5:6 So after they had done all this,
Much fish their nets were snaring.
So great a quantity was caught,
Their fishing nets were tearing.

5:7 They waved for help to their partners
Who were in the other boat.
They filled both ships so full of fish
That they could not stay afloat.

5:8 Simon Peter saw this and cried,
Falling down at Jesus's knees,
"O Lord, since I'm a sinful man,
Depart from my presence please!"

5:9 For he and all his companions
Were so overwhelmed with awe
Because of all they gathered in,
The great catch of fish they saw.

5:10 Now with Simon were the partners,
Known as the Sons of Thunder,[50]
Zebedees' sons named James and John.
They too were filled with wonder.

But Jesus commanded Simon,
"Do not be afraid again.
From this time on your work will be
Catching not fish[51] but men."

5:11 After the boats were brought to land
By each of the fishermen,
They left all industry behind,
And followed Jesus then.

5:12 While He was in one of the towns,
This incident came to be.
Behold, before Him was a man
Who was full of leprosy.

For when he recognized Jesus,
He fell facedown and implored,
"If You have the desire," he cried,
"You can make me clean, O Lord!"

5:13 So reaching out to the leper,
Jesus touched him with His hand.
"I am willing to make you clean.
So be cleansed!" He did command.

Instantly the leprosy left,
5:14 But then Jesus warned the man
Not to tell any person yet
But to listen to His plan.*

"When you leave, go straight to the priest.
Your whole body let him view,
And bring an offering for cleansing
As Moses commanded you.

"Let that be your testimony
To the people everywhere.
First, let the priest declare you clean.
Then your healing you can share."[52]

5:15 The news of Him spread even more,
And great crowds this news did yield.
They wished not only to hear Him
But wished also to be healed.

5:16 Because the crowds became so big,
He would often slip away
Into the deserts by Himself
And would spend time there to pray.

5:17 One day when Jesus was teaching,
There among the crowd He saw*
Many Pharisees sitting there,
Also teachers of the law.

From every town in Judea,
Every town in Galilee,
And also from Jerusalem,
These had come to Him to see.

Now Jesus Himself was holding
The great power of the Lord
For the healing of all the sick
So that they could be restored.*

5:18 Then behold, some men were trying
To bring a paralyzed man
Whom they were hauling on a bed,
For his healing was their plan.[53]

5:19 But to make their way past the crowd,
They were unable to do.
So they went up on the housetop.
The tiles they lowered him through.

They let him down into the crowd
As he lay upon his bed
And placed him in front of Jesus,
5:20 Who observed their faith and said:

"Friend, your sins are forgiven you."
5:21 But the scribes and Pharisees
Began to reason by saying,
"Who's this that speaks blasphemies?

"Who is able to forgive sins?
There is only one who can.
This power belongs to that One,
To God, not to any man."

5:22 Now Jesus knowing their thinking,
Answered back with this reply,
"You all are thinking in your hearts,
But tell Me the reason why?

5:23 "Which is much easier to say
Between these two kinds of talk:*
'Your sins have been forgiven you,'
Or to say, 'Get up and walk?'

5:24 "But concerning the Son of Man,
So that you may learn this fact:
Forgiveness of sins on the earth
He has power to transact."

To the paralytic He said,
"I command you now to rise.
Pick up your cot. Go to your home."
And he rose to their surprise.[54]

5:25 For instantly the man got up.
There was not any delay.
Carrying his cot, he went on home,
While praising God all the way.

5:26 Being gripped with astonishment,
The crowd started praising God.
"We've seen amazing things today,"
They said being overawed.

5:27 Now after this Jesus went out,
And a person caught His eye,
A tax collector in his booth,
A man whose name was Levi.

He said to Levi, "Follow Me."
5:28 So then Levi did just that.[55]
Just leaving everything behind,
He got up from where he sat.

5:29 A big feast for Him in his home,
Levi decided to throw.
A great crowd of tax collectors
And many others did show.

As these were sitting down with them,
5:30 There arrived another lot.
The Pharisees came with their scribes,
And they were greatly distraught.

Muttering to His disciples,
His action they did condemn,*
"Why tax collectors and sinners,
Why eat and why drink with them?"

5:31 Jesus answered and said to them,
"A doctor helps those in need.*
It's not to the well but the sick
That a doctor must pay heed.

5:32 "I've not come to call the righteous.
For that work I was not sent,*
But sinners I have come to call,
To call sinners to repent."

5:33 And then they pointed out to Him,
"These men often fast and pray,
Pupils of Pharisees and John,
But Yours eat and drink each day."

5:34 But Jesus answered back to them,
"Guests of the bridegroom abound.[56]
You would not make his guests to fast
While the bridegroom is around.

5:35 "One day he will be snatched from them.
Their time with him will be past,*
And when the bridegroom is taken,
In those days his guests will fast."

5:36 He continued to speak to them
As this parable He told,
"No one tears from a new garment,
And sews it on one that's old.

"For this tears up a new garment
In order to make a patch,*
And the piece torn from this garment,
With the old one it won't match.

5:37 "And new wine into old wineskins,
Who would ever dare to pour?
For the new wine would burst the skins
And spill out onto the floor.

"Aside from wasting the new wine,
The wineskins would be destroyed.
5:38 In fresh skins new wine must be poured,
Its destruction to avoid.*

5:39 "And after drinking wine that's old,
No one would desire new wine.
For this person would surely say,
'It's the old that's very fine.'"

6:1 He was going through some grain fields
On a certain Sabbath day.
His disciples who were with Him
Were gleaning along the way.

They were picking and eating grain
As within their hands they cracked,
6:2 But some Pharisees questioned them
In objection to this act.*

"It is not lawful to do this
Since this is a Sabbath day.
Why do you do unlawful things
And not live the Sabbath way?"*

6:3 Jesus said in reply to them,
"About this have you not read,
What David and those with him did
When hungering for some bread?

6:4 "Have you not read about this case,
How he went into God's home
And took the consecrated bread
That was for the priests alone?

"Have you not read that David ate
What was unlawful to eat
And gave the bread to those with him
For their hunger needs to meet?"*

6:5 Jesus then conveyed this reply
To the ones whom He addressed,
"The Son of Man, yes, He is Lord,
He's Lord of the Sabbath rest."

6:6 Now on another Sabbath day
Another event occurred.
Jesus entered the synagogue
And was teaching them God's word.

A man with a shriveled right hand
Happened to be present there,
6:7 And the scribes and the Pharisees
Of this man were much aware.*

They were watching Jesus closely
To accuse Him on good grounds.
They wondered if He'd heal this day
And cross the Sabbath day bounds.

6:8 Jesus knew what they were thinking
And so issued this command:*
"Get up and come up front," He said
To him with the shriveled hand.

The man got up and came up front.
6:9 Then Jesus said to the crowd,
"I ask you what's the lawful deed?
What has the Sabbath allowed?*

"Is it lawful on the Sabbath
To do good or to do ill?
Is it lawful on the Sabbath
To save a life or to kill?"

6:10 After looking at all of them,
"Stretch out your hand!" said the Lord.
The man did just as he was told,
And his hand, it was restored.

6:11 But the scribes and the Pharisees,
Their fury just grew and grew.
So they discussed among themselves
What to Jesus they should do.

6:12 Now in those days it came about
That to a mountain He went
With the purpose to pray to God,
And all night in prayer He spent.

6:13 When day dawned, His disciples came
Because of His beckoned call.
He named apostles among them,
Choosing twelve of them in all:

6:14 Simon, whom Jesus named Peter,
Also his brother, Andrew,
Zebedees' sons, named[57] James and John,
Philip and Bartholomew.

6:15 Jesus chose Matthew and Thomas,
Alphaeus's son, named James,
And Simon known as the Zealot.
Then Jesus picked two more names.*

6:16 He picked Judas, the son of James,
And one more Judas He chose.*
It was Judas Iscariot,
Who as a traitor arose.

6:17 Coming down with His apostles,
He stood on a level place.
A great crowd of His disciples
Were gathered before His face.*

Many others were gathered there.
From these regions came this host:
All Judea, Jerusalem,
Also Tyre and Sidon's coast.

6:18 They had traveled to hear Him speak,
And be healed of their diseases.
Those troubled with unclean spirits
Were all being healed by Jesus.

6:19 Now all the crowd was pressing Him,
For power from Him did come.
He was healing those who touched Him,
Healing each and every one.

6:20 Then turning to His disciples,
From His mouth these words did flow.
With His eyes fixed upon them all
Came words of blessing and woe:*

"Those of you who are destitute,
How blessed you all are indeed,
For to you belong God's kingdom,
Great riches beyond your need.*

6:21 "And those of you who now hunger,
How blessed you all are inside,
For you will be completely filled,
Yes, completely satisfied.*

"Those of you who now weep with grief,
How blessed you all are as well,
For you will be so comforted[58]
That laughter in you will dwell.

6:22 "How blessed are you when men hate you,
When you they insult and ban,
When they smear your reputation
Because of the Son of Man.

6:23 "In that day leap up and be glad.
Your reward in heaven is great,
For their ancestors did the same.
The prophets they did berate.

6:24 "But woe to you who now are rich,
Who think that you have no need,*
For now you have all you will get.
Your comfort you have indeed.

6:25 "Woe to you who are now well-fed,
For hunger in you will prevail.
Woe to you who presently laugh,
For you all will mourn and wail.

6:26 "Woe to you when this comes about,
When all men speak of you well,
For their ancestors did the same.
Their praise on false prophets fell.

6:27 "But I say to you who listen,
Love to enemies express.
6:28 Practice good toward those who hate you.
As for those who curse you, bless.

"And pray for those who mistreat you.
6:29 Revenge you must never seek.*
If one slaps one side of your face,
Just offer the other cheek.

"Whoever takes away your coat,
That one you must not attack.*
If he wants your inner garment,
Then from him do not hold back.

6:30 "Give to all who demand from you,
And if from you one should steal,
Do not keep demanding it back,
Regardless of how you feel.*

6:31 "You all want to be treated right*
By everyone that you meet.*
As you want to be treated right,
In like manner you must treat.

6:32 "If you just love those who love you,
What kind of grace do you give?
For just loving those who love you
Is the way the sinners live.

6:33 "And if you restrict your good deeds
To just those who treat you well,
Then what kind of grace do you give
Since in this sinners excel?

6:34 "If you just lend to certain ones,
To the ones who will repay,
Then what kind of grace do you give
Since sinners lend in this way?

"For when sinners lend to sinners,
Their intent is to reclaim.
Whatever amount they lend out,
They require back the same.

6:35 "Love your enemies and do good.
If you lend, do it this way:
Expecting nothing in return.
Do all this just as I say.*

"You'll show yourselves as sons of God,[59]
And you will receive great gain.
On evil and ungrateful men
Benevolence God does rain.

6:36 "So practice being merciful.
Deeds of mercy you must do.*
As your Father is merciful,
So you be merciful too.

6:37 "And judging others, do not do,
And judgment you will not see.
If you do not condemn others,
Your punishment will not be.

"And if you keep on practicing
Forgiving those wronging you,
Then you'll also be forgiven
Of all the wrongs that you do.*

6:38 "Give and it will be given you.
Into your lap they will pour
A measure that is just as great
As that which you gave before.*

"'Twill be pressed down, stirred together,
Overflowing all about,
For by your standard of measure,
To you they will measure out."

6:39 Now He told them a parable,
"These conditions I submit.*
If a blind man leads a blind man,
Won't they both fall in a pit?

6:40 "A student has his own teacher,
But above him he is not,
Yet he will be like his teacher
When he has been fully taught.

6:41 "Now you quickly note the splinter
That is in your brother's eye,
Yet do not note the log in yours.
I command you, tell Me why.

6:42 "How can you say to your brother,
'Let me take that splinter out!'
When you can't see within your eye
The log that is sticking out?

"You hypocrite, *unblock your eyes.
First remove the log that's there.
Then you'll see in your brother's eye
To rid the splinter with care.

6:43 "Does a good tree produce bad fruit,
Or a bad tree bear what's great?
There is not even one such tree
Possessing this kind of trait.*

6:44 "Every tree is known by its fruit,
And to reap like this, men can't:
By picking figs from thorn bushes
Or grapes from a brier plant.

6:45 “The good man has within his heart
A storehouse full of good things,
And from that storehouse in his heart
Those good treasures this man brings.

“But not so of the evil man.
Wickedness he does impart
Because his mouth can only speak
From the things that fill his heart.

6:46 “Why do you call to Me, ‘Lord, Lord,’
Yet practice not what I say?
Why do you call Me by this name*
When My words you don’t obey?*

6:47 “I will show you what one is like
Who comes to Me in this way,
Who listens to the words I speak
And acts on the words I say.

6:48 “He’s like a man who builds a house,
Preparing the earth with care.*
He dug deep until rock he found
And laid the foundation there.

“Then when a flood happened to come,
The house the flood could not tilt.
The waters could not move the house
Because it had been well built.

6:49 “But as for him who hears My words,
Yet them he does not obey,
I will show you what he is like
Who lives not the way I say.*

"He's like a man who built a house,
Setting it upon the ground,
Having no foundation at all,
And so making it unsound.*

"So when the waters crashed the house,
It collapsed right then and there.
It could not stand against the flood,
And was ruined beyond repair."

7:1 After completing all His words
Before the people's hearing,
He then went to Capernaum
Where one heard of His appearing.*

7:2 A slave of a centurion
Was sick and about to die.
The centurion valued him.
His respect for him was high.

7:3 So when he heard about Jesus,
Some Jewish elders He sent
To ask Jesus to heal his slave,
And so this company went.*

7:4 This company came to Jesus
And diligently beseeched,
"Please grant this man what he requests,
For worthiness he has reached.

7:5 “This man has demonstrated love
Toward our Jewish nation.
He built for us our synagogue.
He’s won our admiration.”*

7:6 So with the elders Jesus went,
But while approaching the place,
The centurion did not feel
Worthy to receive His face.[60]

So he sent out some of his friends
To tell Jesus in his stead,
“Sir, no longer trouble Yourself.
Take no further steps ahead.*

“I’m unworthy for You to come
Under my very own roof.
7:7 I’m unworthy to come to You.
That is why I stand aloof.*

“I know that if You speak the word,
My sick servant will be healed,
7:8 For I too am a man who knows
To authority one must yield.

“I’m one under authority,
Having soldiers under me.
If I say to this soldier, ‘Go!’
Then he goes as I decree.

“If I say to another, ‘Come!’
Then he comes just as I say,
And if I tell my slave, ‘Do this,’
Then my words he does obey.”

7:9 When Jesus had heard all these words,
At his faith He was amazed.
He turned to the crowd trailing Him,
And to them his faith He praised.*

"I say to every one of you,
This kind of faith I've not found,
Not even throughout Israel.
This man's faith is so profound."

7:10 After the ones who had been sent
Journeyed back into the place,
They found the slave all healed and well.
The sickness had left no trace.*

7:11 He went into a town called Nain
Soon after this incident.
A large crowd was along with Him.
His disciples also went.

7:12 And as He neared the city gate,
A procession* they all eyed,
And there was being carried out
A man who had somehow died.

He was his mother's only son,
And her husband too had died.
A great crowd from the town did walk
With the mother as she cried.

7:13 Pity for her filled the Lord's heart.
So to the mother He said,
"You can stop weeping for your son."
7:14 Then He approached the coffin bed.

He gently touched the coffin bed.
To a stop the bearers came.
"Young man, I say to you, get up!"
The Lord Jesus did exclaim.

7:15 The dead man started speaking words,
Sitting up, as Jesus said.
Jesus gave him to his mother
By raising him from the dead.*

7:16 At first they all were gripped with fear,
But then God they each one praised.
"God has visited His people.
A great prophet He has raised."

7:17 Now this report concerning Him
Spread through the Judean land,
In all the surrounding places,
"He's a prophet with God's hand."*

7:18 John's disciples brought before John
A report of what occurred.
7:19 John then summoned two disciples,
Entrusting them with a word.

He told these two to ask the Lord,
"Are You the Coming One,
Or should we seek another man?"
Then he sent them to God's Son.[61]

7:20 When the men found Jesus, they said,
"From John[62] a question we've got.
Are You the One who is to come,
Or should another be sought?"

7:21 Now He cured many that same hour
From burdens* of every kind,
From illness, plagues, evil spirits,
And healed many who were blind.

7:22 To the two men He then replied,
"Return to John with this word.
Report to him all that you've seen,
And tell him all that you've heard.

"The blind do see. The lame do walk.
The lepers are lepers no more.
The deaf do hear. The dead are raised.
The gospel is preached to the poor.

7:23 "He who does not trip over Me,
This person is truly blessed."
7:24 When the two[63] left, He spoke of John.
To the crowd He then addressed:

"Into the desert you all went,
But what did you go to see,
A reed being swayed by a wind?
Is that what you hoped him to be?

7:25 "Or did you go to see a man
In clothing finely designed?
Men of luxury dress that way.
In palaces these you'll find.

7:26 "A prophet did you go to see?
I tell you he's so much more.
7:27 He's the one of whom is written
In prophecy long before.

"'See My messenger whom I send
Ahead of Your very face.
He will prepare the road for You.
Ahead of You him I'll place.'

7:28 "Among all those born of women,
Greater than John there is none.
Yet the least born in God's kingdom
Is much greater than this one."

7:29 When all the people heard these words
(Even tax collectors too),
Submitting to John's baptism,
They declared God's way as true.

7:30 But the Pharisees and lawyers,
God's plan for them they despised.
Seeing no need for repentance,*
They refused to be baptized.

7:31 "To what, therefore, will I compare
The men of this generation?
What is a similarity?
What is a correlation?

7:32 "They're like children who are sitting
In the marketplace to play,
Calling out to one another
To do whatever they say:

"'We played the flute for you to dance,
But dancing you would not do.
We sang a dirge for you to weep,
But you would not heed our cue.'*

7:33 "For John the Baptist came this way:
He consumed no wine nor bread.
Yet you say, 'He's demon-possessed!'
And then what else have you said?

7:34 "The Son of Man both eats and drinks.
You say, 'Look at whom He befriends.
He's a glutton and a drunkard.
He's with sinners and publicans!'

7:35 "And wisdom has been justified
By her children, all of them.
Look at the wisdom you've instilled*
In this generation of men."*

7:36 One Pharisee was begging Him
To come to his house and dine.
So Jesus came into his house
At the table to recline.

7:37 A woman in the town who was
A sinner by reputation
Learned that Jesus was in that house
And came without invitation.[64]

An alabaster jar she brought,
Filled with perfume fine and sweet.
7:38 As He reclined at the table,
She stood behind by His feet.

She then began to weep so much,
On His feet her tears just dropped.
She knelt[65] down with her head of hair,
And His wet feet she then mopped.

With tears she kept kissing His feet,
And mopping them with her hair.
Then she poured out perfume on them
From the jar she had brought there.*

7:39 When the Pharisee who had begged
Jesus to come to his home
Saw the woman do all of this,
To himself he then did groan:

"If this Man were a prophet true,
He would most certainly know
What kind of woman this one is,
A sinner who touches Him so."

7:40 But Jesus answered back to him,
"Simon, I have words for you."
Simon replied, "Speak them, Teacher."
This lesson He did construe.*

7:41 "This creditor had two people
Who owed him much money yet.
Five hundred days' wages one owed,
Fifty was the other's debt.

7:42 "But both of them could not repay.
So he forgave the debts they bore.
Now which of the two, would you think,
Would love the creditor more?"

7:43 Simon, replying, said, "I guess
The person forgiven more."
Jesus said, "Your judgment is right."
7:44 Then turned to her on the floor.

He said to Simon about her,
"This woman here do you see?
Although I came into your home,
What custom did you do for Me?[66]

"You gave no water for My feet.
For My feet you did not care,*
But she has wet them with her tears
And has wiped them with her hair.

7:45 "You gave Me no kiss when I came,
The customary way to greet,*
But since the time I have come in,
She's not stopped kissing My feet.

7:46 "And with the common olive* oil
You did not anoint My head,
But this one anointed My feet
With costly perfume instead.

7:47 "Because of this, I say to you
Her sins, though many they be,
All of them have been forgiven,
For she showed much love to Me.

"The one whose sins are forgiven,
Whose sins number few as such,
Since the forgiveness will be small,
That one will not love as much."

7:48 Then to the woman Jesus said,
"Your sins are forgiven you."
7:49 Those who were reclining with Him
Discussed and then questioned too.

"Who's this that forgives even sins?"
7:50 But to her Jesus did say,
"The faith you displayed has saved you.
Now in peace be on your way."

8:1 Now some time after this event,
He was going from town to town,
Also from city to city,
Proclaiming news all around.

The good news which He was preaching
Concerned the kingdom of God.
The Twelve were traveling with Him.
8:2 Many women joined the squad.

Some were women who had been healed
Of illnesses that they had.
Some were women who had been healed
Of spirits evil and bad.

There was Mary called Magdalene
From whom seven demons were thrown.
8:3 Joanna, the wife of Chuza
(As Herod's steward he was known).

And there was also Suzanna
And many more women there
Who were serving His basic needs.
By their own means they did share.

8:4 While a large crowd was gathering,
Who from cities all around
Were traveling to see Jesus,
A parable He did expound.

8:5 "A sower went to sow his seeds.
Some fell by the road somewhere.
Those seeds were trampled underfoot,
Consumed by birds of the air.

8:6 "On rocky ground other seeds fell,
But as soon as they did sprout,
They withered away drying up,
For moisture they were without.

8:7 "Now among thorns other seeds fell,
And as plants from these did sprout,
The thorns grew up along with them
And then choked the plants right out.

8:8 "Onto good ground other seeds fell,
And from these seeds plants had grown,
Bearing fruit one hundred times more
Than the others that were sown."*

As Jesus said all of these things,
These words He'd loudly convey,
"Anyone who has ears to hear
Keep listening to what I say."

8:9 Though His disciples were listening,*
With this they were not content.*
So they began questioning Him
Just what this parable meant.

8:10 He said to them concerning this,
"To know what's hidden from view,[67]
The mysteries of God's kingdom,
This gift has been given you.

"But to the rest, in parables
The mysteries they will receive.
So though they see, they may not see.
Though hearing, they may not perceive.

8:11 "This is what the parable means:
The seeds represent God's word.
8:12 The ones that fell beside the road
Are the people who have heard.

"But then the Devil comes along
And takes from their heart God's word
So that they may not come to faith
And be saved by what they heard.

8:13 "The ones that fell on rocky ground
Are the ones who, when they hear,
Receive the word of God with joy
With no root to hold it dear.

"Though outwardly they do believe,
That time is not long at all.
When times of testing come along,
Away from God's word they fall.

8:14 "The ones which fell among the thorns,
These too are those who have heard,
But as they go on with their lives,
No place is found for God's word.*

"Their lives are choked with worrying
As riches become their pursuit.
Pursuing pleasures of this life,
They yield no maturing fruit.

8:15 "And those which fell on the good ground
Are those with hearts good and fair,
Who've heard the word and hold it fast,
And enduring fruit they bear.

8:16 "Not one person would light a lamp
And then cover it with a jar
Or hide the lamp under a bed.
This practice would be bizarre.*

"But when a person lights a lamp,
On a stand it finds a place.
That way all those who enter in
Can see the light for that space.

8:17 "For there's nothing that is hidden
That won't someday be revealed.
All will be known and come to light,
Even secrets now concealed.

8:18 "So be careful how you listen,
For when all things are revealed,[68]
Those who have will be given more,
For lasting fruit these did yield.*

"So be careful how you listen,
For when all goes on display,*
Those who don't have but think they have,
That, too, will be snatched away."

8:19 Now Jesus's mother and brothers
Were trying to make their way,
But they weren't able to reach Him
Because of the crowd that day.

8:20 So a report was brought to Him,
"To see You, Lord, is the will
Of Your mother and Your brothers
Who are standing outside still."

8:21 He then answered and said to them,
"My mother and brothers are they
Who listen to the word of God
And practice it and obey."

8:22 Now to His disciples He said
(In those days this came about),
"Let's go to this lake's other side."
They boarded a boat and launched out.

8:23 And as they were sailing along,
Jesus fell into a sleep.
Then a strong windstorm came right down.
Across the lake it did sweep.

They were being swamped by the storm.
The danger was very great.
8:24 They came to Jesus, woke Him up,
Fearing death to be their fate.*

"Master! Master! We're perishing!"
Waking Him up by their shrill.
He rebuked the wind and the waves,
Which stopped, and then all was still.

8:25 He said to them, "Where is your faith?"
They were filled with fear and awe.
They were saying to each other
Because of what they just saw:[69]

"Who is this that can do such things,
Who can make storms go away,*
Who commands the winds and the waves
So the elements obey?"

8:26 And then they continued sailing
To the land across the sea,
To the region called Gerasenes
Right across from Galilee.

8:27 When Jesus stepped onto the land,
There appeared a man undressed
Who was from the nearby city,
Who by demons was possessed.

For quite a lengthy span of time
Without clothes this man had gone.
He was not living in a house.
To the tombs he had withdrawn.

8:28 When seeing Jesus, he cried out,
And before His feet he fell.
Then in a voice extremely loud
This utterance he did yell:

"Jesus, Son of the Most High God,
With You I have nothing to do!
Please do not come and torture me.
I beg and I plead with You!"*

8:29 For to the spirit in the man,
The unclean spirit inside,
Jesus ordered to exit out
From the man it occupied.

For it had seized him many times,
And though chained (both hands and feet),
And though he was kept under guard,
The spirit these would defeat.*

As the unclean spirit seized him,
He would break apart his chains,
And then the demon would drive him
Out into the desert plains.

8:30 Jesus asked him, "What is your name?"
"My name's Legion," he replied,
For many demons had entered
And within him did abide.*

8:31 The demons were entreating Him
Not to issue the command
That they all go to the abyss
When departing from the man.

8:32 A herd of many pigs were near.
On the mountain they were feeding.
The demons wished to enter them,
And this they were entreating.

They came out and entered the pigs
8:33 When Jesus allowed them to go.
The herd rushed down the sloping bank
And drowned in the lake below.

8:34 When the ones who tended the herd
Witnessed how the pigs had died,[70]
They ran away, reporting it
In the town and countryside.

8:35 Many came to see what happened,
And to Jesus they were drawn.
At His feet they found one sitting
From whom the demons had gone.

They noticed he was wearing clothes
And saw he was thinking right.
The changed condition of this man*
Filled all the people with fright.

8:36 But the ones who had witnessed this,
These fearful ones they did tell
How he who had been demonized
Had been made completely well.

8:37 So all the people who did live
Around the locality
Of the region called Gerasenes
Asked Jesus to leave them be.

They begged of Him to go away.
Great fear was gripping their heart.
So Jesus got into a boat,
And from them He did depart.

8:38 The man from whom the demons went,
With Jesus he wanted to stay.
He was begging to go with Him,
But Jesus sent him away.

8:39 Jesus said, "Return to your house.
Tell the great things that occurred.
Describe what God has done for you.
Return now and spread this word."*

The man complied and went away.
Through the whole town *he did run,
Announcing all the mighty things
That Jesus for him had done.

8:40 In the returning of Jesus,
A multitude had amassed.
All were expecting His return.
Warm welcomes on Him they cast.

8:41 Now a synagogue official,
Or Jairus, as he was known,
Came and fell down at Jesus's feet,
Begging Him to enter his home.

8:42 For he had an only daughter
Who was about twelve years old,
And she was dying at his home.
So to his house Jesus strolled.

But as He went, the multitudes
Were pressing on every side,
Making it difficult for Him*
To progress with every stride.*

8:43 A woman with a hemorrhage
Of the incurable kind,
Who for twelve years had been bleeding,
8:44 Approached Jesus from behind.

She touched the edge of His garment,
And at once the flow did stop.
What no one was able to cure,
By a touch no blood did drop.*

8:45 "Now who is the one that touched Me?"
Jesus began to survey.
As all denied being the one,
To Jesus, Peter did say:

"O Master, this mass of people
Are just crowding in so much
And pressing in on every side.
It just felt like someone's touch."*

8:46 But Jesus said, "I know for sure
That some person touched Me so.
I felt power come out of Me
A very short time ago."*

8:47 When the woman saw she could not
Escape His accusation,
She came and fell down at His feet
In fear and trepidation.

In the presence of all the crowd,
Her actions she then explained,
Why she touched Him and the result,
The instant cure she had gained.

8:48 "O daughter," Jesus said to her,
"It is faith that you display.*
You've been cured because of your faith.
Now in peace be on your way."

8:49 Now while Jesus was still speaking,
A man came with news to tell
From the synagogue leader's home
The fate his daughter befell.*

"No longer trouble the Teacher,
For your daughter, she has died."
8:50 When Jesus heard what had been said,
To Jairus He then replied:

"Stop letting this fill you with fear.
Do not listen to this word.*
If you just have faith and believe,
Then your daughter will be cured."

8:51 When Jesus arrived at the house,
To enter He let no other
Except for Peter, John, and James,
And the girl's father and mother.

8:52 Now all were grieving over her.
They lamented and did weep.
But Jesus said to them, "Don't cry.
She's not dead but just asleep."

8:53 They all began to laugh at Him,
Certain that the girl had died,
8:54 But He took the child by the hand,
"My child, now get up!" He cried.

8:55 Her spirit returned. She got up
Instantly at His request.
He then instructed that some food
Be given her to digest.

8:56 Her parents were amazed by this,
But He warned them not to tell,
Not to speak to any person
How their daughter was made well.[71]

9:1 When calling the Twelve together,
He gave them authority,
Power over all the demons,
And healing ability.

9:2 Concerning the kingdom of God,
He sent them all out to tell.
He also sent them out to make
All the sick completely well.

9:3 "For this journey," He said to them,
"Don't take what one might suppose,*
No staff or bag, no bread or coins,
Not even two sets of clothes.

9:4 "And whatever house you enter,
That is where you are to stay.
Then go from there throughout the town
To minister every day.*

9:5 "For those who give you no welcome,
This word against them you make.
As you are leaving from that town,
The dust from your feet you shake."

9:6 So they departed on their way.
From town to town they were sent,
Preaching good news to everyone,
Healing everywhere they went.

9:7 News of all that was happening,
To Herod the tetrarch spread.
He was greatly troubled because
Of the words that were being said.

Some were saying concerning John
That he was raised from the dead,
But Herod replied, "I myself
Had someone cut off his head."

9:8 Some said Elijah had come back
As the prophets had foretold.[72]
Some said there had come back to life
One of the prophets of old.

9:9 Herod kept trying to see Him,
Not satisfied with these views
After asking, "Who is this man,
About whom I hear such news?"

9:10 Now when the apostles returned,
Before Jesus they did come
And gave to Him a full account
Of everything they had done.

Then Jesus taking them with Him,
Walked privately on a route
To a city called Bethsaida,
9:11 But of this the crowds found out.

And when they had caught up to Him,
He welcomed them with this word,
Speaking to them of God's kingdom,
And those who had need He cured.

9:12 As the day was nearing its end,
The Twelve to Him did suggest,
"Send the people away from here
That they may find food and rest.

"For we are in a desert place,
But in the towns that surround,
Also throughout the countryside
Lodging and food can be found."

9:13 But Jesus replied to the Twelve,
"You give them something to eat!"
They said, "With five loaves and two fish
We can't accomplish this feat.*

"Unless we go and buy the food,
Enough food for all of them."
9:14 (For there were about five thousand,
And that's just counting the men.)

So He said to His disciples,
"Have them all gather around
And sit in groups of fifty each."
9:15 They obeyed and sat them down.

9:16 He took the five loaves and two fish
And looked up into the sky.
He blessed the food by giving thanks.
Then broke up the food supply.

He kept giving the disciples
From the food that was supplied
To distribute to the people,
9:17 Who ate until satisfied.

Now all the leftover fragments
The disciples[73] then obtained
By putting them into baskets,
And twelve basketsful remained.

9:18 Now some time after this event
When just His disciples were there,
Jesus came to inquire of them
After being alone in prayer.

"Who do the crowds say that I am?"
Jesus began to survey.
9:19 "Some think You are John the Baptist,
Or Elijah, others say.

"But others think You're someone else,
One of the prophets of old
Who has come back to life again.
These are the views that they hold."*

9:20 "But who do you say that I am?"
Was Jesus's second question.
"You are the Christ, the King[74] from God,"
Was Peter's prompt confession.

9:21 But Jesus sternly warned them all
To tell no one of that phrase,
And then He said, "The Son of Man
Must suffer in many ways.

9:22 "By the elders, chief priests, and scribes,
The Son must be rejected.
He must be killed, but the third day
He will be resurrected."

9:23 Then He was saying to them all,
The disciples and the crowd,[75]
"He who wishes to follow Me,
Let himself be disavowed.

"Then take up your cross every day,
And keep on following Me,
9:24 For all who wish to save their lives
Will lose their lives totally.

"But all who wish the opposite,
For My sake their lives to lose,
They will actually save their lives
Since My life is what they choose.*

9:25 "For if the whole world one should gain,
What profit is in this prize
If in the course of doing that
He forfeits himself and dies?

9:26 "One day the Son of Man will come
In His glory for all to view,
In the glory of the Father,
Of the holy angels too.

"If someone is ashamed of Me,
Ashamed of the words I say,
The Son[76] will be ashamed of him
When He comes again that day.

9:27 "Some of those who are standing here
(I tell you this truthfully)
Will not taste death in any way
Until God's kingdom they see."

9:28 Now after Jesus said these words,
About eight days' time had gone.
Up the mountain He went to pray,
Taking Peter, James, and John.

9:29 Now sometime while He was praying,
Something happened that was strange.*
His clothes became extremely white,
And His facial form did change.

9:30 Behold, Moses and Elijah,
9:31 In glory they did appear,
Speaking with Jesus of His death
That was drawing very near.

These two men discussed with Jesus
Of the death He would fulfill,
Occurring in Jerusalem,
A departure by His will.*

9:32 Now Peter and his companions
Did not see this from the start,
For sometime during His praying
Into sleep they did depart.

But when they did become awake,
His bright glory they did view,
And they saw standing with Jesus
Some men, specifically two.

9:33 Now sometime later when these men
From Him were about to leave,
Peter just spouted out these words
Which showed that he was naïve.

"Master, it's good that we are here.
Three tabernacles will do,
One for Moses and Elijah.
And let us make one for You."

9:34 And while he was still saying this,
Before them a cloud appeared
That came and overshadowed them,
And entering the cloud they feared.

9:35 Then a voice that came from the cloud
Proclaimed, "This is My Son.
You must listen to what He says,
For He is the Chosen One."

9:36 When the voice had finished speaking,
Just Jesus was standing there,
And in those days they told no one.
What they saw they did not share.

9:37 Sometime later on the next day,
After making their descent
From the mountain where He had prayed,
A great crowd to Jesus went.

9:38 From the crowd a man shouted out,
"Teacher, examine my son.
I'm begging You to look at him
Since he is my only one.

9:39 "Behold, a spirit seizes him,
And he suddenly cries out.
It throws him into convulsions,
With much foaming at the mouth.

"The spirit hardly leaves him,
Bruising my one son a lot.
9:40 I begged these men to cast it out.
Your disciples, they could not."

9:41 Jesus answered and said these words,
"O faithless generation,
How long must I remain with you,
O crooked population?

"How long must I put up with you?"
And then He addressed the man,[77]
"You get your son and bring him here."
He submitted to this plan.*

9:42 Now while the son was coming near,
The demon just threw him down,
Putting him into convulsions,
Making him roll all around.[78]

But Jesus rebuked the demon,
The spirit that was unclean.
He healed the boy and gave him back
To his father at the scene.

9:43 All were amazed at God's power,
But while marveling at His deeds,
Jesus turned to His disciples
And gave them these words *as seeds:

9:44 "Let these words sink into your ears.
You'll hear them again and again.*
The Son of Man will be betrayed,
Given to the hands of men."

9:45 His words they did not understand.
The meaning had been obscured
So that they would not comprehend,
And they dared not ask a word.

9:46 Now as they were discussing things,
There arose an argument
About which of them was greatest,
Resulting in great dissent.

9:47 The reasoning within their heart
From the Lord they could not hide.[79]
So Jesus took a little child
And stood the child by His side.

9:48 "Receiving this child in My name
Is receiving Me in that sphere.
Whoever is receiving Me
Receives Him who sent Me here.

"Now that you have heard this lesson,*
You can settle your debate,*
For he who is least among you,
That is the one who is great."

9:49 John responded, "Master, we saw
Someone else using Your name
As he was casting out demons.
So to stop him was our aim.

"We kept on trying to stop him*
From doing this ministry*
Since he does not follow along,
Along with our company."

9:50 “Stop preventing such work as that,”
To his words Jesus replied,
“For he who is not against you
Consider as on your side.”

9:51 Now sometime later as the days
Were nearing for His ascension,
To travel to Jerusalem
Jesus fixed His attention.

9:52 He sent before Him messengers
Who went ahead to prepare
In a town of Samaritans
His future arrival there.

9:53 But when He came into the town,[80]
The people welcomed Him not
Because toward Jerusalem
Was the journey He had sought.

9:54 When His disciples saw all this,
Specifically John and James,
They said, “O Lord, what do You wish?
Shall we now call down some flames?

“Shall we command that fire come down,
Down from the heaven above,
And consume these Samaritans
Who welcomed You not with love?”*

9:55 But Jesus turned, rebuking them,
And answered, "You do not know
What kind of attitude you have,
What kind of spirit you show.

9:56 ["For the Son of Man did not come
To destroy the lives of men,
But for this reason He has come
To rescue their lives from sin."][81]

So to another town they went,
9:57 And as they were on their way,
"Wherever You go, I'll follow,"
A man to Jesus did say.

9:58 "Foxes have holes and birds have nests,"
To this same man Jesus said,
"But nowhere has the Son of Man
A place to lay down His head."

9:59 Jesus turned to another man.
"You follow Me," He coerced.
But this man said, "Please let me go
And bury my father first."

9:60 But Jesus replied to this man,
"Let the dead bury their dead,
But as for you go and proclaim
The kingdom of God instead."

9:61 Now another man also said,
"O Lord, I will follow You,
But let me first go to my home
And bid my household adieu."

9:62 But Jesus replied to this man,
"That's walking a crooked track,*
For none are fit for God's kingdom
Who plow as they're looking back."

10:1 After these things the Lord did count.
Seventy more He did choose.
He sent them to each town and place.
He sent them ahead in twos.

Wherever the Lord planned to go
And minister with His grace,*
He first would send ahead of Him
The seventy to that place.

10:2 And He was saying to these ones,
"The harvest is great, 'tis true,
But the workers for this harvest
Are in number very few.

"So ask the Lord of the harvest.
Make it a matter of prayer.*
Request that into His harvest
He would send out workers there.

10:3 "Get going, but take careful note,
That as lambs I send you out.
I send you in the midst of wolves
With nothing to carry about.[82]

10:4 “Carry no purse, no bag, no shoes.
Greet nobody on your way.
10:5 Whatever house you enter in,
‘Peace to this household,’ first say.

10:6 “And if a son of peace is there,
Upon him your peace will rest,
But if there is no son of peace,
’Twill return to you, *the blessed.

10:7 “Now do not move from house to house,
But in that one house you stay.
Eat and drink what they give to you,
For the worker deserves his pay.

10:8 “And whatever town you enter
That welcomes you in with care,
Eat what is set in front of you,
10:9 And heal the sick that are there.

“Say to those who are in those towns
Who welcome you when you appear,
Say to them, ‘The kingdom of God
To you has come very near.’

10:10 “But whatever town you enter
That declines to welcome you,
Go out into its streets and warn
With these words and actions too:*

10:11 “‘Even the dust of your city
Which unto our feet adhere,
We shake against you, but be sure
That God’s kingdom has come near.’

10:12 "I say to you that in that day
That Sodom will tolerate
Its judgment much more easily
Than that city's dooming fate.

10:13 "O Chorazin and Bethsaida,
How horrible it will be
For you on the day of judgment
For the miracles you see.

"For if the miracles you see
Were in Tyre and Sidon wrought,
They'd be in sackcloth and ashes.
Repentance they long would have sought.

10:14 "But it will be more tolerable
For Sidon and for Tyre,
For when the day of judgment comes,
Your judgment will be higher.

10:15 "And as for you, Capernaum,
Will you be lifted up high,
Raised to the heavens above?
No! In Hades you will lie.

10:16 "The one who listens to your words
Gives their ear to Me as well,
For I have sent you seventy*
So that My words you will tell.*

"He who rejects you rejects Me.
Also God they don't revere*
Because the one who rejects Me
Rejects Him who sent Me here."

10:17 The seventy returned with joy,
And to Him they did exclaim,
"Lord, even the demons are forced
To submit to us in Your name."

10:18 And He said to them, "I saw him
Falling from heaven on high.
I was observing Satan fall
Just like lightning from the sky.

10:19 "To tread on scorpions and snakes,
I've given you power to exert
Over all the enemy's power,
And nothing will bring you hurt.

10:20 "However, don't rejoice in this,
That to you the spirits comply.
But instead rejoice that your names
Are written in heaven on high."

10:21 In that same hour which He spoke,
Jesus abounded with bliss.
Joyful in the Holy Spirit,
He publicly* then prayed this:

"Father, Lord of heaven and earth,
From the intelligent and wise
You've hidden what You've shown to babes.
Yes, 'twas pleasing to Your eyes.

"I praise You Father for just that."
Then He said after this prayer,*
10:22 "All things have been given to Me
By My Father who's up there.

"And no one really knows the Son,
Personally,* I mean to say.
No one but the Father, that is,
Truly knows the Son in this way.

"No one really knows the Father
Except for the Son, He knows,
And anyone to whom the Son
Determines to disclose."

10:23 Then turning to His disciples,
He said to them privately,
"How blessed are the eyes of the ones
Who view all the things you see.

10:24 "I say many prophets and kings
Desired to see what you view
And desired to hear what you hear,
But this none of them could do."

10:25 Now a certain lawyer stood up
To put Jesus to the test,
"If I'm to gain eternal life,
Teacher, what must be my quest?"

10:26 Jesus replied with a question,
"What is written in the Law?
How does what's written read to you?
What conclusion do you draw?"*

10:27 He replied, "Love the Lord your God
With all your soul and your heart,
With all your strength and all your mind.
Love Him fully not in part.*

"And just as you would love yourself,
To your neighbor love you give;"
10:28 Jesus said, "Your answer is right.
Do all this, and you will live."

10:29 Wishing to justify himself,
To Jesus the lawyer said,
"Who is considered my neighbor?
Interpret this law we've read."*

10:30 Jesus answered, "A certain man
Was traveling to Jericho,
Coming down from Jerusalem,
A dangerous route to go.*

"Into the hands of thieves he fell
Who stripped him of all his clothes.
They went off leaving him half dead
After giving him many blows.

10:31 "It so happened a certain priest
Was traveling down that road,
But when he saw the half-dead man,
On the other side he strode.

10:32 "A Levite, too, was traveling,
And seeing him in that place,
He passed by on the other side,
Continuing with his pace.*

10:33 "A traveling Samaritan
Came upon him where he lay,
And when he saw him he was moved
To care for the man that day.

10:34 "He came up to the half-dead man.
All his wounds in cloth he dressed,
Poured olive oil and wine on them,
Using up what he possessed.*

"On his own beast he placed the man,
Transporting him to an inn,
And there he took care of the man.
He did, a Samaritan!*

10:35 "The next day he drew out some coins
From that which he did carry
And gave them to the innkeeper.
They were worth two denarii.

"He said to him, 'Care for this man,
And if it should cost you more,
Upon my return to this place,
Your money I will restore.'

10:36 "Now which of these men do you think
As a neighbor proved to be
To the man who fell among thieves,
Which do you think of these three?"

10:37 "The one who showed mercy to him,"
He said, *omitting that name.[83]
Then Jesus said to the lawyer,
"You go and do just the same."

10:38 Now in the course of their journey,
Into a town Jesus came.
A woman opened her home to Him,
And Martha was her name.

10:39 She had a sister named Mary,
Who absorbed the words He said.
Now she was sitting at His feet.
10:40 Martha was serving instead.

Since much serving was to be done,
To Jesus she did object,
"Lord, is it no concern of Yours
That Mary is in neglect?*

"My sister has abandoned me
And left me with every task.
Tell her to help me with the work.
Lord, this is all that I ask."*

10:41 "Martha, Martha," the Lord replied,
"Worries and burdens you carry.
You fill your mind with many things
10:42 When few are necessary.

"Only one is necessary,
And the good part Mary chose.
This will not be removed from her.
I won't do what you propose."*

11:1 Now it happened sometime later
That Jesus withdrew in prayer.
While praying in this certain place,
His disciples too were there.

After He had finished praying,
One presented Him this thought,
"John told his pupils how to pray.
Lord, please teach us as John taught."

11:2 "When you pray," Jesus said to them,
"Say, 'O Father, let Your name
Be set apart and sanctified
In all that we might proclaim.*

"'And let Your kingdom soon arrive,
11:3 And provide for us our bread,
Enough to meet our daily needs,
For by Your hand we are fed.*

11:4 "'And forgive our sins, all of them.
Cancel all the debt we owe,*
Since to those indebted to us
Forgiveness we do bestow.

"'And do not lead us down the road
Into temptation's snare.'
These are the topics to cover
Whenever you are in prayer."[84]

11:5 Then He went on to illustrate,
"Let's suppose you have a friend.
You go and ask him at midnight,
'Three bread loaves to me please lend.

11:6 "'A friend of mine has come to me
From a journey he has made,
Yet I've no food to offer him.
Therefore, friend, I need your aid.'

11:7 "But from inside the friend will say,
'Stop bothering me this night.
Already the door has been shut.
The door is now locked up tight.

"'My children and I are in bed.
Three bread loaves I cannot bring.*
I cannot get up out of bed
And give to you anything.'

11:8 "I tell you that he won't get up
Just because he is his friend
And give him anything at all
That his friend wants him to lend.

"I tell you the man will get up
If with persistence he pleads.
Yes, he'll get up and give to him
Just as much as his friend needs.

11:9 "So I say to you keep asking,
And you will surely receive.
Keep on seeking, and you will find.
To persistence you must cleave.*

"And if you keep right on knocking,
The door will become unlocked.
It will be opened up for you,
You who persistently knocked.*

11:10 "You see, all who ask will receive,
And all those who seek will find.
All who knock the door will open
If persistently designed.[85]

11:11 "Suppose some father among you
Were asked for a fish by his son,
Would he give him a snake instead?
No father would do this, not one![86]

11:12 "Or what if he asks for an egg?
What gift would his father bestow?
Would he give him a scorpion?
Would his father do this? No!

11:13 "Since you know how to give good gifts
To your own son or daughter,
Since you being evil do this,
What of your heavenly Father?

"How much more is it true for Him,
Your Father who has no sin,*
That He'll give the Holy Spirit
To those who keep asking Him."

11:14 There was a demon that was dumb
Whom Jesus was casting out.
As the demon left the dumb man,
Some words he began to spout.

The crowd of people were amazed,
But some possessed no belief.*
11:15 Some just said, "He casts out demons
By Beelzebul, their chief."

11:16 But other people tested Him,
Insisting by His own hand
That He perform a miracle
From heaven on their demand.

11:17 But Jesus knew their inner thoughts,
And so this wisdom He boomed:
"Any kingdom that's divided
Against its own self is doomed.

"House upon house will just collapse,
11:18 And so how can Satan gain*
If divided against himself?
How will his kingdom remain?

"You say that I cast out demons
By the might Satan supplies.[87]
11:19 So if this were true, then by whom
Do all your sons exorcise?

“Therefore, they will be your judges,
11:20 But if God’s finger this is from
Whenever I cast out demons,
Then God’s kingdom to you has come.

11:21 “When a mighty man fully armed
Keeps guard over his own home,
Each and everything that he has
Is kept safe and left alone.

11:22 “But when someone stronger attacks,
The owner he does subdue.
He steals the armor trusted in,
And divides the spoils too.

11:23 “Anyone who is not with Me
Is against Me in all matters.
He who does not gather with Me,
In everything he scatters.

11:24 “Whenever the unclean spirit
Exits a man it possessed,
It passes through desert places
And seeks out some place to rest.

“But when it cannot find a place,
‘I’ll return,’ the demon speaks,
‘Back to my home from which I came.’
Its last home the demon seeks.*

11:25 “When it arrives, it finds the home
Neatly swept and in décor.
11:26 It then seeks out seven spirits,
But their evil is much more.

"It brings the spirits to the home,
And they enter to live there.
The last state of that man is worse
Than his first state of despair."

11:27 From the crowd, as He spoke these words,
A woman gave this outburst,
"How blessed is the womb that bore You,
And the breasts where You were nursed."

11:28 Jesus responded with these words:
"How so much more blessed are they
Who listen to the word of God
And the word of God obey."

11:29 Now as the crowds greatly increased,
Jesus began to speak out,
"Wicked is this generation,
For a sign it does seek out.

"But no sign will be given it,
Not one sign it wants done,
But only the sign of Jonah
Will be given by the Son.

11:30 "For just as Jonah was a sign
To the Ninevite nation,
The Son of Man will be a sign
To this wicked generation.

11:31 "The Queen of the South will rise up
Along with this generation,
And when that time of judgment comes,
She'll announce its condemnation.

"For to hear Solomon's wisdom,
She came from a distant place.
Look! One greater than Solomon
Is right here before your face.

11:32 "The Ninevite men will stand up
Along with this generation.
And when that time of judgment comes,
They'll announce its condemnation.

"For the Ninevites repented
After Jonah preached God's word.
But look! One greater than Jonah
Stands before you to be heard.

11:33 "No one, after lighting a lamp,
Hides the light from people's view,
Or puts it under a basket.
This not one person would do.*

"But everyone who lights a lamp
Will put the lamp on a base
So that people may see the light,
Those who come into that place.

11:34 "Now your body's lamp is your eye.
Whenever your eye is sound,
Your total body will be lit.
With the light it will abound.

"Yes, your body's lamp is your eye,
But when your eye is unsound,
Your total body will be dark.
With darkness it will abound.

11:35 "Because of this, be on your guard
So that the light within you
May not be actually darkness,
But is a light that is true.*

11:36 "So if your whole body is light
With no darkness in its blaze,
It will be all lit like a lamp
That shines on you with its rays."

11:37 Now at the time of this teaching,
A Pharisee did request
That Jesus eat a meal with him,
And He entered as his guest.

He reclined right at the table,
11:38 Not washing before He ate,
And when the Pharisee saw this,
Great surprise it did create.

11:39 The Lord said, "O you Pharisees,
Take great care in this matter.
You clean the outside of the cup
And also of the platter.

"But on the inside you are filled
With wickedness and with greed;
11:40 Did not He who made the outside
Make the inside too? Indeed![88]

"You are very foolish in this,
11:41 But if you give alms from within,
Then for you everything is clean.
You are not guilty of sin.*

11:42 "But woe to all you Pharisees,
For you tithe your mint and rue,
And every kind of garden herb,
But this you do not pursue:

"You do not pursue fair judgment.
You do not pursue God's love,
But these are what you should have done
Along with the tithe thereof.

11:43 "Yes, woe to all you Pharisees,
For you love the front-row seat,
Facing those[89] in the synagogues
Who have gathered there to meet.*

"You also love the greetings made
Directed to your faces
Which you hear as you walk around*
Throughout the marketplaces.

11:44 "Yes, woe to all you Pharisees.
Like hidden tombs you compare.
The people walk right over them,
Being wholly unaware."[90]

11:45 One of the lawyers said to Him,
"Teacher, these words you project
Insult us too since some of us
Belong to that Jewish sect."[91]

11:46 But Jesus replied with these words:
"Woe to you lawyers as well,
For you weigh people down with weights
By the rules that you compel.[92]

"The burdens you put on others
Are too difficult to bear.
To touch these weights with one finger,
None of you would even dare.

11:47 "Woe to you for the things you do.
The tombs of prophets you build.
What prophets do you do this for?*
The ones whom your fathers killed.

11:48 "You witness and approve the deeds
Which your ancestors fulfilled
Since they put to death the prophets.
So those prophets' tombs you build.

11:49 "For this reason, God's wisdom said,
'I will send to them these men,
My prophets and my apostles,
And they will kill some of them.

"'Some of them they will put to death,
And some they will persecute
11:50 So that to this generation
This judgment I will impute:

"'The blood of all the prophets shed
From the time of creation,
11:51 From Abel to Zechariah,
Is on this generation.

"'Zechariah was killed between
The altar and sanctuary.
Yes, against this generation,
The charge for his blood they'll carry.'

11:52 "Woe to you lawyers for stealing.
The key to knowledge you hide.
You did not even enter in,
And you hindered those who tried."

11:53 When Jesus went out from the house,
Great hostility arose.
Both the scribes and the Pharisees,
Many questions they did pose.

They attacked Jesus with questions
About many things that day,
11:54 Plotting to trap Him in something
That He might happen to say.

12:1 Now in this time of questioning,
The multitude did abound.
Thousands stepping on one another
As they all gathered around.

He first spoke with His disciples,
"On your guard you all must be.
Watch out for the Pharisees' yeast
Which is called hypocrisy.

12:2 “Now there is nothing covered up
That will never be revealed,
And nothing that will not be known
That is secret and concealed.

12:3 “Whatever you’ve said in the dark,
In the light it will be heard.
What you’ve whispered in private rooms
Will become a public word.[93]

12:4 “To you, My friends, I say to you,
Do not be afraid of men
Who kill the body, for afterward,
They can bring no harm again.

12:5 “But I will warn you whom to fear.
Fear the one who has the might
To cast into hell after death.
Yes, to fear Him, I incite.

12:6 “Don’t five sparrows cost two small coins?
Yet by God none are ignored.
12:7 Even all the hairs on your head
Have been counted by your Lord.

“So there’s no need to be afraid.
Great worth you all have indeed.
Compared to numerous sparrows,
Your value it does exceed.

12:8 “I tell you, all who confess Me
Before the presence of men,
The Son of Man will confess him
Before all God’s angels then.

12:9 “But anyone who denies Me
Before the presence of men,
That one will also be denied
Before all God’s angels then.

12:10 “Now those who speak an evil word
That’s against the Son of Man,
That sin will be forgiven him.
That transgression will not stand.*

“If against the Holy Spirit
One speaks a blasphemous word,
That sin won’t be forgiven him.
His judgment he has incurred.*

12:11 “Before synagogues and rulers
And before authorities,
You will be brought for questioning,[94]
But worry not about these.

“Don’t worry about your defense,
About the things you should say,
Or how you are to speak your words.
Don’t worry in any way.*

12:12 “For in that very time you’re asked
To present your own defense,
The Holy Spirit will teach you
All the words you must dispense.”

12:13 Someone said to Him from the crowd,
“Teacher, *come to my defense.
Tell my brother to split with me
The family inheritance.”

12:14 But Jesus replied to this one,
"Man, who put Me in this place
That I should be judge over you,
Arbitrator of this case?"

12:15 Then Jesus told them, "Guard yourselves
From each of the forms of greed.
For a man's life is not defined
By abundance. So take heed!"

12:16 Jesus told them this parable:
"There was this very rich man
Whose land produced so many crops
That he had to plot and plan.*

12:17 "And reasoning within himself,
He asked, 'What am I to do?
For I don't have any more room
To store the crops I just grew.'

12:18 "Then he thought, 'This is what I'll do:
All of my barns I will raze.
I'll build bigger barns for my grain
And my goods for the coming days.

12:19 "'And then I will say to myself,
Many goods your barns carry.
Relax. You're set for many years.
Eat and drink and be merry!'

12:20 "But then God said to him, 'You fool!
This very night you will die.
Now who will own what you've prepared?
Who will now get your supply?'

12:21 "So it will be for anyone
Who for his own self does store
All the treasures he has obtained,
But whose heart toward God is poor."

12:22 Then He said to His disciples,
"Therefore, you all I entreat.
Stop being anxious for your life
As to what you are to eat.

"Don't worry about your body
As to what clothing on you goes,
12:23 For life is so much more than food,
And the body much more than clothes.

12:24 "Now just think about the ravens.
Neither do they sow nor reap.
They have no private storehouses
Or buildings for food to keep.

"God keeps on feeding the ravens.
Therefore, because this is true,*
How much greater value than birds
Have every one of you.

12:25 "Which one of you can add more time
To your life by being stressed?
12:26 Since you can't do this smallest thing,
Why worry about the rest?

12:27 "Think about how the lilies grow.
They don't work or make their clothes.
Yet Solomon in all his glory
Clothed himself like none of those.

12:28 "Today the grass is in the field.
Tomorrow it will be tossed
Into the furnace to be burned.
All its beauty will be lost.*

"So since God clothes the grass this way,
In the splendor that we view,*
O people, you of little faith,
How much more will God clothe you!

12:29 "Therefore, do not keep on seeking
The things you might eat or drink.
Stop your worry about these things.
Stop thinking like pagans think.*

12:30 "For all the nations of the world
After these eagerly chase.
Your Father knows you need these things.
12:31 On His kingdom set your face.

"Yes, keep on seeking His kingdom,
And if on that you do dwell,*
All these things the world seeks after
Will be given you as well.

12:32 "O little flock, there is no cause
To fill yourselves up with fright
Because to give you the kingdom
Is your Father's great delight.

12:33 "Sell what you own, your possessions,
And then take all the proceeds,[95]
Give it away to charity
To those who truly have needs.

"Make yourselves eternal purses,
Purses that never wear out,
Unfailing treasure in heaven,
Where no thief can lurk about.

"Make yourselves eternal purses,
Purses that never decay,
Unfailing treasure in heaven,
Where no moth can eat away.[96]

"Make yourselves eternal purses,
Purses that don't fall apart,
12:34 For wherever your treasure is,
There also will be your heart.

12:35 "Be all dressed and ready to go
At anytime day or night,
And don't forget to hold your lamps
And keep them all burning bright.

12:36 "Be like men waiting for their lord
From a marriage celebration
So that they open when he knocks
Without any hesitation.

12:37 "Slaves are blessed when their lord comes
If alertness he does observe.
Truly he'll sit them down to eat
And ready himself to serve.

12:38 "Whether the second or third watch
Be the time that he arrives,
If the lord finds his slaves alert,
How happy will be their lives.

12:39 "If the house owner would have known
When the thief's coming was due,
Be assured he would not have let
His house be broken into.

12:40 "So you too be on the alert,
Always ready and expect*
Because the Son of Man will come
At a time you don't suspect."

12:41 "To whom, O Lord, do you address
This parable that You tell?
Do You speak to us?" Peter asked,
"Or to everyone as well?"

12:42 The Lord said, "Who is the steward
That is both faithful and wise
To whom his master will entrust
His servants and his supplies?

"That steward is in charge of food
To measure and to assign
To all the servants in the house
At the designated time.

12:43 "When his lord comes and finds him thus,
How happy that slave will be.
12:44 Truly, I say he'll give that slave
All of his own property.

12:45 "But suppose that slave says in his heart,
'My lord won't come for some time,'
And beats the male and female slaves,
And feasts and gets drunk with wine.

12:46 "That slave's lord will come on a day
Before the slave will prepare.
That slave's lord will come at a time
Of which he is unaware.

"The lord will cut him in pieces
And assign him to a place
Along with all the unfaithful
Who looked not for the lord's face.*

12:47 "And that slave who knew his lord's will,
But readiness he did leave,
And acted against his lord's will,
Many stripes he will receive.

12:48 "But he who did not know his will,
And wrong deeds he did pursue,
Deeds deserving of a beating,
Will receive only a few.

"From all who have been given much,
Then much will be required.
From those to whom are charged with much,
Then more will be desired.

12:49 "I came to throw fire on the earth.
How I wish it were ablaze.
12:50 I've a baptism to receive.
How heavy on Me this weighs.

"That which I'm to be baptized with,
Over this I am distressed,
And until that is accomplished,
I will not have any rest.*

12:51 "Do you think to give peace on earth
Is the reason for My life?
No, I tell you, My coming here
Does not bring peace but strife.

12:52 "For in a home that numbers five,
From now on strife there will be,
Three against the other two
And the two against the three.

12:53 "That household will be divided,
The father against his son,
The son against his own father.
Harmony will not be won.*

"And the mother of the household,
Against her daughter she'll be,
The daughter against her mother,
Only strife, no harmony.*

"The mother-in-law will be against
Her daughter-in-law, I tell.
The daughter-in-law will be against
Her mother-in-law as well."

12:54 He was also telling the crowds,
"You're quick and right to maintain
That when a cloud forms in the west
That it is going to rain.

12:55 "And when the wind comes from the south,
'It will be hot,' you all say.
And sure enough, as predicted,
It turns out hot that same day.

12:56 "Hypocrites! You know to discern
The face of the earth and sky.
How is it that to this season
Discernment you don't apply?

12:57 "And why don't you judge what is right?
Why not this initiate?
12:58 For you work to settle lawsuits
To avoid the magistrate.

"While going with your opponent
To appear before the court,
You instigate a settlement
So his action he'll abort.

"Or else he'll drag you to the judge
So his justice will prevail.*
The judge will give you to the bailiff
Who will throw you into jail.

12:59 "I tell you, you won't be released
From this, your imprisonment,
Until you have paid all you owe,
Up to the very last cent."

13:1 At this same time some informed Him
That some Galileans were slain,
And Pilate had mingled their blood
In the offerings with which they came.

13:2 Jesus said in response to them,
"Do you think their sins were great,
Worse than other Galileans
Because they suffered this fate?

13:3 "I tell you, no, that is not true,
And so unless you repent,
You will as these Galileans
Suffer horrible judgment.

13:4 "Or what about this incident,
The eighteen who had been crushed
When the Siloam tower fell
And its walls upon them rushed?

"Do you suppose that they were killed
Because their offenses were great,
Worse than all in Jerusalem
Who did not suffer this fate?*

13:5 "I tell you, no, that is not true,
And so unless you repent,
You will, as these eighteen did,
Suffer horrible judgment."

13:6 Then speaking to that very crowd,
This parable He began:
"A fig tree planted in a vineyard
Was owned by a certain man.

"He came to look at the fig tree
To see how much fruit it bore,
But he did not find any fruit
Just like the two years before.[97]

13:7 “So to the gardener he then said,
‘For the last three years I’ve come
Looking for fruit on this fig tree,
But each time I have found none.

“‘Cut it down! For why should it waste
The ground it is planted in?’
13:8 ‘Let it be, sir, for one more year,’
The gardener replied to him.

“‘Let me dig around the fig tree,
And on it manure throw.
13:9 If it bears fruit next year, then great,
But if not, then it can go.’”

13:10 Now in one of the synagogues
(On a Sabbath day this fell),
Jesus was teaching when He saw
A woman *who was not well.

13:11 For eighteen years by a spirit
She was in a weakened state.
She was bent over severely,
Unable to stand up straight.

13:12 Jesus called her to come to Him.
“Woman,” to her He conveyed,
“From this weakness you are released.”
13:13 Then on her His hands He laid.

Immediately she straightened up
At the touch of Jesus's hand.
She began to glorify God
Because straight she now could stand.*

13:14 The ruler of the synagogue
Was enraged by this display
Since Jesus had performed this deed,
Working on the Sabbath day.

"Six days are set aside for work,"
The ruler to all appealed,
"So come on any of those days,
Not the Sabbath, to get healed."

13:15 The Lord replied to him and said,
"You are hypocrites, I say.
For don't each one of you do this,
Working on the Sabbath day?

"The donkey or the ox you free,
Taking it out from the stall.
Then leading it, you water it.
Who does this work? But you all!*

13:16 "Now this is Abraham's daughter.
For eighteen years—Satan's prey.
Satan bound her. Why not free her
On this Sabbath day?"

13:17 His opponents were put to shame
While these words He was voicing,
And for the great things done by Him,
The whole crowd was rejoicing.

13:18 Then He said, "The kingdom of God,
To what thing shall I compare?
What illustration can I use?*
13:19 A mustard seed, I declare.

"Yes, it is like a mustard seed
That a person took and threw,
Putting it in his own garden,
And the seed just grew and grew.

"Then when that seed became a tree,
The birds of the sky did nest
Within the branches of the tree,
Possessing a place to rest."*

13:20 And again He said, "God's kingdom,
To what thing shall I compare?
What illustration can I use?*
13:21 It is like yeast, I declare.

"It's like yeast that a woman took
And mixed it in with some wheat,
About sixty pounds of flour meal[98]
'Til its raising was complete."

13:22 He was going through cities and towns,
Advancing from place to place,
Progressing toward Jerusalem
While teaching about God's grace.[99]

13:23 And someone said to Jesus, "Lord,
Will few receive salvation?"
So He answered, addressing them,
"Make this your aspiration:

13:24 "Strive to go through the narrow door,
For many, I say to you,
Many will seek to enter in
But will not be able to.

13:25 "For once the owner of the house
Has risen and shut the door,
You'll stand outside and start to knock.
The owner you will implore.

"'Lord, open up the door for us!'
You will bellow *with no shame,
But he will answer back to you,
'I know not from where you came.'

13:26 "You'll then begin to say to him,
Supposing that he forgot,*
'We ate and drank in your presence,
And in our streets you have taught.'

13:27 "But he will say, 'I tell you all,
There is no excuse, just blame.*
Depart from me, evildoers.
I know not from where you came.'

13:28 "There will be eyes dripping with tears;
There'll be teeth gnashing with pain
When you see those in God's kingdom,
But His kingdom you did not gain.

"Abraham, Isaac, and Jacob,
There, you will see them reside.
You will see all the prophets there,
But you will be thrown outside.

13:29 "People will come from all around,
From the north, south, west, and east.
Yes, they will come to God's kingdom
And will partake in the feast.

13:30 "Behold, the last, who will be first,
And the first, who will be last.
You will see this in God's kingdom*
As outside you all are cast."*

13:31 At this same time some Pharisees
Came up to Jesus and said,
"Go away and depart from here,
For King Herod wants You dead."

13:32 He said to them, "Go tell that fox,
'Take notice of what I do.
I cast out demons, and I heal
Today and tomorrow too.

"'But the third day I'll reach My goal.
On this goal My eyes are fixed.'*
13:33 Yet I must journey on today,
tomorrow, and then the next.

"For outside of Jerusalem
A prophet can't possibly die.
13:34 Jerusalem, Jerusalem,
You've given the wrong reply!*

"You kill the prophets, and you stone
All those whom to you were sent.
To gather your children as one,
How often was My intent.

"For just as a hen would gather
All her chicks under her wings,
I wished to gather your children,
But you would not have these things.

13:35 "Behold, your house is left to you.
My presence you'll not afford
Until you say, 'Blessed is He
Who comes in the name of the Lord.'"

14:1 Sometime later, on a Sabbath
When He went to eat a meal
In a ruling Pharisee's house,
They watched for Him to heal.[100]

14:2 And right there in front of Jesus
Was a man with a disease.
From dropsy he was suffering,
Swelling up to great degrees.[101]

14:3 From the lawyers and Pharisees
An answer Jesus then sought,
"Is it lawful on the Sabbath
To heal one who's sick or not?"

14:4 But they did not reply to Him.
Not one answer did they say.
So He took the man and healed him.
Then He sent the man away.

14:5 Then He asked them, "Which one of you,
If upon a Sabbath day
Your son or ox fell in a well,
Would not rescue right away?"

14:6 No lawyer and no Pharisee
Could come up with a reply.
His reasoning did silence them.*
His logic none could deny.*

14:7 He was telling a parable
To those invited to eat
After seeing how they picked out
The chief places as their seat.

14:8 "When you're invited by someone
To come to a wedding feast,
The seat of honor do not take,
But the seat that's for the least.[102]

"Someone may have been invited
Much more important than you.
If you're in the seat of honor,
14:9 Here is what the host will do:

"He will come and will say to you,
'Give to this man your place.'
Then in the least place you will sit
As you go there in disgrace.

14:10 "So when invited by someone
To come to a wedding feast,
The seat of honor do not take,
But the seat that's for the least.

"For then the host will come and say,
'Friend, move to a better seat,'
And you'll have honor before all
Who are with you there to eat.

14:11 "For all those who exalt themselves,
A low place they will acquire,
But the one who humbles himself,
He will be raised up higher."

14:12 The host who had invited Him,
Jesus expressly addressed,
"When you give a luncheon or feast,
Be careful who is your guest.

"Do not give an invitation
To friends, no, not at all,
Not your brothers or relatives,
And rich neighbors do not call.

"If you invite any of them,
They just might have this concern,*
That when they choose to have a feast,
To invite you in return.

"And so you then will be repaid
By these because they're able.
You invite them; they in return*
Invite you to their table.*

14:13 "But when you give a reception,
Invite the poor and the blind.
Invite the crippled and the lame.
Invite people of these kind.*

14:14 "You'll be blessed because repayment
They can't possibly achieve.
When the righteous are raised to life,
Repayment you will receive."

14:15 One man who was dining with Him,
Hearing this, to Jesus said,
"How blessed is everyone who in
The kingdom of God eats bread."

14:16 But Jesus replied to this man,
"Now there was a certain one
Who was preparing a great feast,
Inviting many to come.

14:17 "And when the dinner time arrived,
His slave he sent out to say
To those who had been invited,
'Come right now without delay.

"'For everything is ready now,'
The slave said to everyone.*
14:18 But with one heart they all began
Giving reasons not to come.

"The first one gave him this excuse:
'A piece of land I have bought.
Consider me excused I beg.
I must go see my plot.'

14:19 "'Five yoke of oxen I have bought,'
Another person addressed.
'Consider me excused I beg.
My oxen I must test.'

14:20 "And then another one did say,
'I'm very sorry, my friend.*
I just got married to a wife,
And so I cannot attend.'

14:21 "The slave returned to his master.
A complete report he gave.
The house owner enraged by this
Gave more orders to his slave.

"'Go out now into the city.
Bring into my house these kind,
The poor in alleys and the streets,
The crippled, the lame, and the blind.'

14:22 "The slave said, 'Master, it is done.
I have carried out your will.*
I have done as you commanded,
But there's more room still to fill.'

14:23 "So the master said to the slave,
'Go with urgency instilled.
Convince those by the roads and trails
That my whole house may be filled.

14:24 "'For among those invited first,
I tell you, I now reveal,
That none of them will even taste
A piece of my banquet meal.'"

14:25 Now walking along with Jesus
Were masses of great degree.
Turning, He stopped and said to them,
"Do you wish to follow Me?*

14:26 "If any person comes to Me
With other priorities,*
He cannot be My disciple.
He must hate each one of these.

"He must hate his own mom and dad,
His wife and his children too,
His brothers, sisters, and his life
If they keep him from being true.*

14:27 "Whoever follows after Me
Without bearing his own cross,
My disciple he cannot be.
He must count all things as loss.[103]

14:28 "For which of you would not do this,
A tower wishing to build:
First sit down and add up the cost
To see if it can be fulfilled?

14:29 "For if one does not first sit down,
The cost being never weighed,
What will happen if he must stop
After the foundation is laid?

"All those who see him building this,
About him they will make fun.
14:30 They'll say, 'This man began to build,
But the work could not be done.'

14:31 "Or what king would not do this first
In meeting another in war:
Sit down and ponder his own strength
To decide if he has more?

"For if he has ten thousand men,
Tell Me, how could he prevail,
If with twenty thousand soldiers
The other king does assail?

14:32 "No, while the other is far off,
A delegation he'd send
To ask for all the terms of peace
That the threat of war might end.*

14:33 "So in light of these examples,
My disciple none can be
Unless he gives up all he owns
And then follows after Me.[104]

14:34 "Therefore, salt is considered good.
Except, if salt has no taste,
How will the salt then be restored?
14:35 It's not even fit for waste.

"It is not useful to the soil.
It only is thrown away.
Anyone who has ears to hear,
Let him hear all that I say."

15:1 Now all of the tax collectors
To Jesus were coming near,
And also all of the sinners
Since Him they wanted to hear.

15:2 But both the scribes and Pharisees,
Him they began to malign,
"This Man, Jesus, welcomes sinners.
With all of them He does dine."

15:3 He responded to their charges
With three parables in one:
Of the lost sheep, of the lost coin,*
And of the prodigal son.*

15:4 "Is there a man among you who,
If he had one hundred sheep
Yet one of them was wandering,
Would not be concerned to keep?

"Would you not leave in the pasture
The ninety-nine sheep behind
And search for the one which is lost
Until that one sheep you find?

15:5 "When the shepherd looks for that sheep
And that sheep he does behold,
In joy he lays it on his shoulders,
Bringing it back to the fold.*

15:6 “And when the shepherd comes back home,
Invitations he extends.
‘Rejoice with me! My sheep I’ve found,’
He tells his neighbors and friends.

15:7 “I tell you that in this same way,
As soon as a sinner repents,
Heaven rejoices over this.
The rejoicing is immense.*

“There’s more joy over one sinner
Who turns from the way he went
Than over ninety-nine righteous ones
Who have no need to repent.

15:8 “Or what sort of woman is there,
If ten silver coins she possessed
Yet loses one coin in her home,
To find it would not be pressed?

“She’d light a lamp and sweep the house,
Carefully searching around.
She’d keep on looking everywhere
Until that lost coin is found.

15:9 “When she has found the coin she lost,
Invitations she extends.
‘Rejoice with me! My coin I’ve found,’
She tells her neighbors and friends.

15:10 “I tell you that in this same way
The rejoicing is immense
In the presence of God’s angels
Over one sinner who repents.”

15:11 Now next He said, "There was this man
Who had two sons, full grown.[105]
15:12 The younger said to his father,
'Give me what is mine to own.

"'Father, give me of the estate
That which is rightfully mine.'
The inheritance he then split
Between the two at that time.

15:13 "Yet not many days after that,
The younger son then decided
To gather his things together
That to him had been divided.

"He journeyed to a distant land,
And he spent there all he had,
Wasting it on excessiveness,
On a lifestyle that was bad.

15:14 "After exhausting all his wealth,
A famine that was so great
Hit the country which he was in,
And needful became his state.

15:15 "So to one of the citizens
His service he did consign.
The man sent him into his fields
To take care of all his swine.

15:16 "Now he was longing to be filled
With pods of the carob[106] plant,
Which was what the swine were eating,
Yet his needs no one would grant.

15:17 "But when he came to his senses,
He thought to himself and said,
'Of my father's hired workers,
How many have plenty of bread?

"'They all have much more than they need
While with hunger I'm dying here.
15:18 I'll arise, go to my father,
And say as I draw near:

"'Father, I've sinned against heaven,
And sin against you, I've done.
15:19 Make me as one of your hired men.
I'm unfit to be called your son.'

15:20 "Rising, he went to his father,
But while he was still far away,
His father was moved with pity
As he saw him who went astray.

"The father ran and embraced him,
And kissed him multiple times.
15:21 But the son said to him, 'Father,
I'm guilty of many crimes.*

"'For I have sinned against heaven,
And sin against you, I've done.
I'm no longer worthy enough
To still be called your son.'

15:22 "But to his slaves the father said,
'Quickly do as I command.
Put on him the best robe we've got,
And put a ring on his hand.

"'Also put sandals on his feet,
15:23 And then get the fattened calf.
Slaughter it so that we may eat
And rejoice in his behalf.

15:24 "'For once this son of mine was dead
But to life again has come.
He had been lost but has been found.
Let's rejoice over my son.'*

"And they began to celebrate,
15:25 But the oldest son was not there.
He was returning from the field
When he heard music in the air.

"As he was coming near the house,
He heard people dancing around.
15:26 So calling one of the servants,
He asked the reason for such sound.

15:27 "The servant gave him this reply,
'Your brother, he has been found.
Your father killed the fattened calf.
His son is back safe and sound.'

15:28 "The oldest son became angry,
And refused to enter the place.
So his father came out to him,
Imploring him face to face.

15:29 "But to his father he answered,
'Take careful notice and look.
Many years I've been serving you.
Your commands I never forsook.

"'Yet you never gave me a goat
To celebrate with my friends.
15:30 But you slaughtered the fattened calf
For who? A son who offends.

"'He who consumed your livelihood
And who spent it all on whores
And then returned with nothing left,
This terrible son of yours.'

15:31 "The father said to him, 'O child,
You have always been with me,
And all that's mine is also yours,
Possessions and property.*

15:32 "'For your brother it was a must
To play music and dance around,[107]
For he was dead yet came to life.
He was lost but has been found.'"

16:1 Now to the disciples also
This parable He conveyed,
"There was a certain wealthy man
Who had a steward he paid.

"But charges were brought before him
That the stewardship was bad,
That the steward was squandering
All that the wealthy man had.

16:2 "The rich man summoned the steward.
'What's this that's been told to me?
Account for all your stewardship.
My steward you cannot be.'

16:3 "The steward then thought to himself,
'Just what will I do today
Because the stewardship from me
My master is taking away?

"'I am not strong enough to dig.
To beg, I am too ashamed;
What am I going to do?' he thought,
And this thought he then exclaimed:*

16:4 "'I realize now what I must do
So that when I am relieved
From the stewardship that I had,
Into homes I'll be received.'

16:5 "He summoned his master's debtors.
He asked the first for an amount.
'How much do you owe my master?
What debt is on your account?'*

16:6 "'One hundred baths[108] of olive oil,'
The first debtor gave his quote.
'Take your bill and sit down quickly
And write fifty on the note.'

16:7 "He summoned another debtor,
And asked him for an amount.
'How much do you owe my master?
What debt is on your account?'*

"'It's one hundred measures[109] of wheat,'
The second one gave his quote.
'Take your bill that reads one hundred
And write eighty on the note.'

16:8 "Now since the unrighteous steward
Was shrewd in settling accounts,
His master could only praise him
For obtaining those amounts.*

"For the sons of this worldly age
Are so much more shrewd, all right,
In relating to their own kind
Than are the sons of the light.

16:9 "I tell you, use unrighteous wealth
To gain many friendly faces
So when it fails they'll welcome you
Into the eternal places.

16:10 "Those faithful in the smallest things,
In great things are faithful too.
Those unjust in the smallest things,
In great things are also untrue.

16:11 "Therefore, if you've been unfaithful
In the money of the unjust,
Then concerning the true riches
Into your hands who would entrust?

16:12 "And if with someone else's things
Unfaithfulness from you pours,
Who do you think will give to you
That which is rightfully yours?

16:13 "No servant can serve two masters.
A dilemma this will create,*
For he will end up loving one,
And the other he will hate.

"For to one he will be loyal.
The other he will despise.
You cannot serve God and money.
Many conflicts will arise."*

16:14 The Pharisees heard all His words,
Each and every single one.
Since they were lovers of money,
Of Him they were making fun.

16:15 Jesus responded to their words,
"You are those who in men's sight
Keep on justifying yourselves,
But God knows your hearts aren't right.

"For on that which men place value,
Things of high estimation,
These things in the presence of God
Are an abomination.

16:16 "You had the Law and the Prophets
Before John began to proclaim.
Now God's kingdom is being preached
As good news since the time he came.

"And all those responding enter
God's kingdom, as you can see,
And how are they entering in?
But enthusiastically![110]

16:17 "Now it is so much easier
For heaven and earth to end
Than for part of the Law to fail,
Even one stroke that's been penned.

16:18 "Each one who divorces his wife
And another that one marries,
Is committing adultery.
Guilt of the Law he carries.[111]

"Each one who marries a woman
Who's been divorced from a man
Is committing adultery,
Which the Law you know does ban.[112]

16:19 "A certain rich man clothed himself
In magnificent array,
In purple cloth and fine linen,
Celebrating every day.

16:20 "But a beggar named Lazarus,
Full of sores from toes to head,
Had been laid at the rich man's gate,
16:21 For he wanted to be fed.

"He longed to be filled with the scraps
That fell from the rich man's table,
But with the dogs who licked his sores
To compete he was unable.[113]

16:22 "Now eventually both men died,
But the beggar, he was carried
To Abraham's breast by angels,
And the rich man he was buried.

16:23 "In Hades the rich man raised his eyes,
Being in painful unrest.
He saw Abraham far away
And Lazarus in his breast.

16:24 "And crying out, he himself said,
'O my father, Abraham,
Pity me and send Lazarus,
For in agony I am.

"'Send him to dip his fingertip
In water to ease my pain,
And touch my tongue to cool it off.
I'm in anguish in this flame.'

16:25 "Abraham said, 'Remember, child,
What your own life used to be
When you received all your good things,
But now you're in agony.

"'Lazarus likewise received things,
But his whole life was severe.
Unlike you,* he received bad things,
But now he's in comfort here.

16:26 "'In addition to all these things,
There is this gulf that is wide,
Which is between all you and us
As a permanent divide.

"'Those who wish to go to you all
Can't cross over the divide,
And nonc of you can comc to us.
That is why the gulf is wide.'

16:27 "The rich man answered, 'Then father,
Please send him to these others,
To the household of my father
16:28 Because I have five brothers.

"'Send Lazarus to warn them all
So that they all may repent,[114]
Or else they'll come to be with me
In this region of torment.'

16:29 "Abraham said, 'They have Moses,
And they have the Prophets too.
Let them hear all that these have said.
This Lazarus need not do.'*

16:30 "He said, 'No, father Abraham,
If someone from death does go
To warn my brothers of this place,
They all will repent, I know.'

16:31 "'If they don't listen to Moses,
And the Prophets,' Abraham said,
'Neither will they be persuaded
By someone raised from the dead.'"

17:1 To His disciples He then said,
"From stumbling blocks none can run.
Occasions for them will occur,
But woe through whom they do come.

17:2 "This person would be better off
In the deep parts of the seas
Than to trip up a little one,
Yes, even just one of these.

"Yes, he would be much better off
If around his neck were hung
A gigantic stone from the mill
And in the sea he were flung.

17:3 "Instruct those in sin to repent,
That is, if he's your brother.
If he repents, forgive him then.
Keep guarding one another.

17:4 "Even if he sins against you
As much as seven times a day,
If he says to you 'I repent,'
Forgive him each time, I say."

17:5 To the Lord the apostles said,
"Give us greater faith we pray!"
17:6 "You need faith like a mustard seed,"
The Lord to them did convey.

"All your commands would be obeyed
By this white mulberry tree,[115]
Even the words, 'Be rooted up,
And be planted in the sea.'

17:7 "If you had a servant who plows
Or who to your sheep does tend,
Suppose he comes in from the field.
Just what words would you extend?

"Which one of you would say to him,
'Come here immediately.
Come to the table and relax.
Come here now and eat with me'?

17:8 "No, you[116] would say, 'Prepare my meal.
My needs be ready to meet.
Serve me until I've had my fill,
And then you can drink and eat.'

17:9 "To his servant one would not give
Any words of commendation
For doing the things commanded,
For doing his obligation.*

17:10 "Thus, when you do the minimum,[117]
Do not think that you are just.*
Say, 'We are worthless servants since
We've done only what we must.'"

17:11 Later He was passing between
Samaria and Galilee
While going to Jerusalem
To engage in ministry.*

17:12 As He entered a certain town,
He was met by leprous men
Who stood far off while meeting Him.
Now in number they were ten.

17:13 They shouted out, "Jesus! Master!
Your mercy on us bestow!"
17:14 When He saw them, He said to them,
"To the priests you all must go.

"Go and present yourselves to them
As the Law of Moses decrees."[118]
Then sometime later on their way
They were cleansed from their disease.

17:15 Only one of them turned around
After seeing himself restored.
While praising God with a loud voice,
17:16 He returned to thank the Lord.

He fell on his face at His feet,
Thanking Him again and again
For the healing he had received,
And he was a Samaritan.

17:17 "Were there not ten men who were cleansed?"
Jesus publicly did say.
"And what about the other nine?
Just where exactly are they?

17:18 "Was there no person who was found
Who turned back to give God praise
Except this one, a foreigner?"
These questions Jesus did raise.

17:19 He then told the Samaritan
Whose faith was now on display,*
"It is your faith that has saved[119] you.
Arise and be on your way."

17:20 Now the Pharisees asked Jesus
His reasoning as to when
The kingdom of God would arrive,
And so Jesus answered them.

"God's kingdom, it is not coming
In a way that one can view,
17:21 Nor will they say, 'Look here or there!'
For look! It is within you!"

17:22 Then He said to His disciples,
"The days will certainly come
When you will long to see the days
Of the Son of Man, just one!

"You will not see those days at all,
17:23 Yet others will say to you,
'Look there! Look here!' But don't depart.
These people do not pursue.

17:24 "The Son of Man's day will be swift,
Yet visible to the eye,*
Just like lightning when it flashes,
Streaking right across the sky.

17:25 "But He must suffer many things
Before His revelation.[120]
First, He has to be rejected
By the present generation.

17:26 "As it happened in Noah's days,
So it will also take place
In the days of the Son of Man,
The time He reveals His face.*

17:27 "For they were eating and drinking,
And they were marrying too.
They were being given in marriage.
They were living as people do.*

"Until Noah entered the ark,
They all were living that way.
And then the flood came suddenly
And destroyed them all that day.

17:28 "In just the same way it happened
In the generation of Lot.
The people were eating and drinking,
Giving judgment not a thought.*

"They were selling goods to others
And buying to meet their needs.
They were building various things
And were also planting seeds.

17:29 "But the day that Lot left Sodom,
Judgment no one could avoid.*
Fire and brimstone rained from heaven,
And all were then destroyed.

17:30 "Likewise it will be just the same
In the time, the very day,
That the Son of Man is revealed,
And there will be no delay.*

17:31 “If one should be on his housetop
With his goods inside the place,
He should not go down to get them
When the Son reveals His face. [121]

“Likewise if one is in the field,
To turn around he must not.
17:32 Learn the lesson of what happened
To the wife of the man, Lot.

17:33 “A person will destroy his life
If to keep it is his goal,
But a person will keep his life
If he loses it, the whole.

17:34 “I say, on that night in one bed,
Two people will be reclined,
But one of them will be taken
And the other left behind.

17:35 “Two women will be together
As harvested grain they grind,
But one of them will be taken
And the other left behind.”[122]

17:37 The disciples questioned Jesus,
“Lord, at what place? Tell us where.”
He said, “The place the carcass is,
The eagles will gather there.”

18:1 Then He told them a parable
About their obligation,
To always pray and not lose heart,
And here's the illustration:

18:2 "There was in a certain city
This one judge *who was severe.
He did not respect anyone.
Even God he did not fear.

18:3 "In that city a widow lived
Who kept giving him this plea:
'Deal out justice on my behalf.
Judge against my enemy.'

18:4 "He was unwilling for a time
To respond to her request,
But at last he said to himself,
'This widow gives me no rest.

"'Even though I do not fear God
Or give anyone respect,
18:5 So that she does not wear me out,
This widow I will protect.'"

18:6 The Lord then pointed out to them,
"What that judge said you must hear.
This unjust judge who did respond
To one who did persevere.*

18:7 "And will not God, for His elect
Who cry to Him night and day,
In the end bring about justice,
Though at length He does delay?

18:8 "I'm telling you, that speedily,
Justice for them He will birth.
But when the Son of Man does come,
Will He find faith on the earth?"

18:9 He told this parable to those
Who in their own selves did trust,
Who treated others with contempt,
But who viewed themselves as just.

18:10 "There were two men who went to pray
Into the temple sector.[123]
One of them was a Pharisee,
The other a tax collector.

18:11 "The Pharisee while standing up,
Concerning himself did pray:
'I am nothing like other men.
God, thank You I'm not this way.

"'Thank You that I'm not like scammers
Who rob others through their fraud,*
That I'm not like adulterers,
Or unjust. I thank You, God.

"'That tax collector over there,
Thank You that I'm not like him.
18:12 I fast twice per week, and I pay
One-tenth of all I bring in.'

18:13 "The tax collector, while standing
At a good distance away,
Was unwilling to lift his eyes
To heaven in order to pray.

"But this man was beating his chest
While to God he was saying,
'God, please have mercy upon me,
The sinner!' he was praying.

18:14 "This tax collector, I tell you,
Not the pious Pharisee,
Went down to his home justified.
Righteous before God was he.*

"So each one who exalts himself
Will be humbled and not praised,
But the one who humbles himself
Will be exalted, yes, raised."

18:15 Now they were bringing to Jesus
Their infants for Him to touch,
But when the disciples saw this,
They scolded them very much.

18:16 But He called for them by saying,
"Don't keep them from coming please,
For the kingdom of God belongs
To all people such as these.

18:17 "Truly I say to all of you,
Whoever does not obtain
God's kingdom like a little child,
God's kingdom he'll never gain."[124]

18:18 A certain ruler came to Him.
"Good Teacher," he did inquire,
"How can I gain eternal life?
To what deeds must I aspire?"

18:19 Then Jesus answered back to him,
"You label Me good, but why?
No one is good except for one,
And that is God, *the Most High.

18:20 "You know what the commandments are.
Let us see how you have done:*
'Do not commit adultery;
Do not murder anyone;

"'Do not bear false testimony;
Do not ever, ever steal;
Honor your father and mother.'
So now what do these reveal?"*

18:21 The ruler said in his defense,
"Since the time I was a youth,
I have obeyed all these commands.
I am telling you the truth."*

18:22 Upon hearing these words from him,
Jesus then answered him back,
"You have done well with these commands,*
But there's one thing you still lack.

"Sell everything that you possess.
Give to those in poverty,
And you'll have treasure in heaven.
And then come and follow Me."

18:23 But when the ruler heard these words,
He became very distressed
Because he was extremely rich,
For great treasures he possessed.*

18:24 "How hard it is for those with wealth
God's kingdom to enter in,"
Jesus began to say to them
As He was looking at him.

18:25 "It's easier for a camel
To go through a needle's eye
Than for the rich to enter in
The kingdom of the Most High."[125]

18:26 And they who heard what Jesus said,
This one question they then waved,
"So how is it be possible
For anyone to be saved?"

18:27 Then Jesus answered back to them,
"Impossible things for men
Are not too difficult for God.
To be saved is possible then."*

18:28 Then Peter said, "Take careful note,
Our sacrifice, let's review.*
We ourselves have left all we own
And have followed after You."

18:29 He said to them, "I speak the truth,
All who for God's kingdom's sake
Have sacrificed the things they have,
In much more will they partake.

"There's no one who for God's kingdom
Has left home, brothers, or wife,
Or his parents, or his children,
18:30 Who won't reap more in this life.

"He'll receive much more in this life
Than everything he did leave,
And in the age that is to come
Eternal life he'll receive."

18:31 Then Jesus took the Twelve aside
And told them, "Take careful note,
We're going to Jerusalem
To fulfill what the prophets wrote.

"Yes, all that has been written down,
The words of the prophets of old,
Will happen in Jerusalem,
Fulfilling what was foretold.

18:32 "For to the Gentiles He will be
Delivered up for a trial.
He'll be mocked, scorned, and spat upon,
18:33 And beaten for quite a while.

"And after they have beaten Him,
Then Him the Gentiles will kill,
But the third day following this,
Rise up the Son of Man will."

18:34 But they understood none of this,
The meaning from them concealed.
They did not comprehend at all
The things that Jesus revealed.

18:35 Later as He neared Jericho,
There sitting down by the road
Was a certain blind man begging
For mercy to be bestowed.*

18:36 Now as the blind man heard a crowd
Passing by his location,
He was asking those in the crowd
What was the situation.

18:37 They said, "Jesus of Nazareth
Is now passing by this way."
18:38 "Jesus, Son of David," he cried,
"Have mercy on me, I pray."

18:39 But those who led the multitude
Were ordering him to cease,
But he kept shouting even more,
"Son of David, have mercy please!"

18:40 Jesus stood still and then ordered
That to Him thc man bc brought.
When the man had come close enough,
Jesus asked him what he sought.

18:41 "What would you have Me do for you?"
Jesus to him did inquire.
"Lord," the blind man replied to Him,
"To see again I desire!"

18:42 Then Jesus said to the blind man
In response to his deep plea,*
"Your faith has saved you; you're restored."
18:43 Immediately he could see.

He began to follow Jesus.
God he also glorified.
The crowd praised God after they saw
This great miracle applied.*

19:1 After entering Jericho,
Jesus was passing right through.
19:2 A man who was called Zacchaeus
Wanted to get a good view.

He was a chief tax collector,
Which means he had oversight,[126]
And so he was extremely rich
19:3 But extremely small in height.

He tried to see who Jesus was,
But his view the crowd did block.
19:4 So he ran on ahead of them
Where he knew Jesus would walk.*

So in order to see Jesus
As He was passing his way,
He climbed a black mulberry tree,[127]
A sycamore, *as some say.

19:5 As soon as Jesus reached that spot,
He looked up and then did yell,
"Hurry, Zacchaeus! Come right down!
Today in your home I must dwell."

19:6 Zacchaeus hurried and came down,
Welcoming Jesus with bliss.
19:7 But when the crowd saw what took place,
They all grumbled about this.

"Jesus has gone to be the guest
Of a man who is despised,*
Of a man who is a sinner,"
They muttered and criticized.

19:8 Zacchaeus stopped, said to the Lord,
"Lord, take careful note of me!
I'll give one half of what I own
To the ones in poverty.

"And if I've cheated anyone
in anything in any way,
I will calculate four times that,
And that to him I will pay."

19:9 Then before his face Jesus said,
"Today salvation has come
To the house of this man because
He, too, is Abraham's son.

19:10 "Indeed the Son of Man has come
For this purpose, which I tell,
To find those who are perishing,
And to rescue them as well."

19:11 Now while they all were focusing,
Hearing this proclamation,
Jesus added a parable,
A kind of illustration.*

He spoke this parable because
Jerusalem He was near,
And the crowd assumed God's kingdom
Was just about to appear.

19:12 So Jesus said, "A certain man
Who was of high and noble birth
Was planning to take a journey
To a distant part of the earth.

"He was going to get a kingdom
In order as king to reign
And then return back to his land
As the land of his domain.*

19:13 "But first he called ten of his slaves
And gave ten minas to them.
He then said, 'Do business with this
Until I return again.'

19:14 "But his citizens hated him.
Therefore, messengers they sent
To state, 'We do not want this man
To rule us to this extent.'

19:15 “Some time had passed when he returned
(And his kingdom he obtained).
Those slaves to whom he gave money,
He summoned to see what they’d gained.

19:16 “The first one appeared explaining,
‘The mina you gave me before,
Which was your mina, O master,
It has multiplied to ten more.’

19:17 “‘Well done, good slave,’ the master said,
‘Ten cities are in your care,
For you’ve proven yourself faithful
In the littlest affair.’

19:18 “The second appeared explaining,
‘The mina you gave me before,
Which was your mina, O master,
It has multiplied to five more.’

19:19 “‘Well done, good slave,’ the master said,
‘Five cities are in your care,
For you’ve proven yourself faithful
In the littlest affair.’[128]

19:20 “Then another came explaining,
‘Master, your mina, behold!
I was keeping it in this cloth,
Reserving it in its fold.

19:21 “‘I did this because I fear you.
As a harsh man you are known.
You take up what you have not placed.
You reap what you have not sown.’

19:22 “The master replied to this one,
‘By the very words you gave,
I will now judge what you have done.
You are such a worthless slave.

“‘You view me to be a harsh man,
And is this what you have known:
I take up what I have not placed?
I reap what I have not sown?

19:23 “‘Then why did you not in the bank
This silver of mine invest
So when I returned I could reap
My silver with some interest?’

19:24 “To the bystanders, he then said,
‘From him take the mina away.
To the one who has ten minas,
Entrust it to him, I say.’

19:25 “But they said to him, ‘O master!
He already has a lot.[129]
He already has ten minas.
Why give him what that man’s got?’*

19:26 “The master replied, ‘I tell you,
Those keeping what I gave before,
Having been faithful over it,*
Will be given even more.

“‘But the person to whom I gave
Who does not put it to use,
Even that which he possesses
Will be taken, *no excuse.

19:27 "'As for these who did not desire
For me over them to reign,
Bring them here. They're my enemies.
In my presence have them slain.'"

19:28 After Jesus had said these things,
He proceeded on His way,
Heading up to Jerusalem
From Jericho that same day.*

19:29 Nearing Bethphage and Bethany,
Near the mount called Olivet,
He sent two of the disciples
For Him a donkey to get.*

19:30 "Enter the town that's facing you,
And as you enter you'll see
A never-ridden colt tied up.
Untie it and bring it to Me.

19:31 "If anyone should ask of you,
'This donkey why have you freed?'
In this way you must speak to them,
'Of this colt the Lord has need.'"

19:32 So those disciples who were sent
Went away into the town.
Everything that Jesus told them
Was exactly what they found.

19:33 As they were untying the colt,
Its owners questioned their deed,
"Why are you untying this colt?"
19:34 "Of the colt the Lord has need."

19:35 So they brought the colt to Jesus,
And on it their clothes they flung.
They mounted Jesus on the colt,
Never ridden and so young.*

19:36 As Jesus proceeded to ride,
The people kept on spreading
Their clothes in the road before Him.
Jerusalem was His heading.[130]

19:37 When He at last came near the place
Where the road makes its descent
Down along the Mount of Olives,
The crowd into praises went.

The whole crowd of the disciples
Began to praise God out loud
For the miracles they had seen.
Joyful shouts rang from the crowd.

19:38 "The One who comes in the Lord's name,
Blessed be this King," they all rang.
"Glory in the highest places,
And in heaven, peace!" they sang.

19:39 Some of the group of Pharisees
Who were in the crowd complained,
"Teacher! Rebuke Your disciples.
Their outbursts must be restrained."*

19:40 But Jesus answered back to them,
"If these people do not shout,
I tell you, if they are silenced,
All the stones will then cry out!"

19:41 As He neared and saw the city,
Over it He wept and cried,
19:42 "If you had just known in this day
The things that make peace abide.

"But now those things that do bring peace
Have been hidden from your eyes,
19:43 For the days will come upon you
When your enemies arise.

"They will build up an embankment,
And then you they will surround.
They'll close you in on every side
19:44 And level you to the ground.

"All this with your children inside,
With no stone remaining stacked
Since you did not realize your time
When God came to interact."[131]

19:45 Jesus entered the temple courts,
Throwing out the sellers there,
19:46 Saying to them, "It is written,
'My house will be one of prayer.

"'But you have made it out to be
A den for robbers instead.
My house will be a house of prayer,'
Just as Isaiah said."[132]

19:47 Now Jesus in the temple courts
Was engaged in teaching each day,
But certain ones were seeking grounds
To put Him to death some way.

The chief priests, scribes, and leading men
Were the plotters of this scheme,
19:48 But they found nothing they could do
Since His words all did esteem.

20:1 Later on, on one of the days,
They approached Him to accuse.
He was teaching at the temple
And was preaching the good news.

The chief priests and scribes with elders
20:2 Questioned Jesus publicly,
"By what power do You do these things?
Who gave You authority?"

20:3 He answered back, saying to them,
"This one question first allow:
20:4 John's baptism, was it from men
Or from heaven? Tell me now."

20:5 So they reasoned among themselves
As to what they might achieve,*
"If we say, 'From heaven,' He'll say,
'Why him did you not believe?'

20:6 "But if we say, 'It was from men,'
Us, all the people will stone,
For as a prophet, by this crowd,
Was surely how John was known."

20:7 So concerning its origin,
They said that they knew no facts.
20:8 Jesus said, "Then I won't tell you
By what power I do these acts."

20:9 To the people this parable
Jesus began to declare:
"A man had planted a vineyard
And leased it to farmers there.

"He journeyed for a lengthy time,
20:10 But when harvest time had come,
He sent a slave to those farmers
To collect fruit from each one.

"But the farmers just beat the slave.
With nothing they sent him back.
20:11 The owner sent another slave,
But that slave they did attack.

"They beat him like the other slave,
Offering him no respect.
They sent him back to the owner.
No fruit could the slave collect.

20:12 "A third slave, the owner then sent,
But him they did not receive;
Like the others, they wounded him
And violently made him leave.

20:13 "The owner of the vineyard thought,
'From them how can I collect?
I will send them my beloved son.
Maybe him they will respect.'

20:14 "But when the farmers saw the son,
They plotted right then and there,
'So this property may be ours,
Let us kill him! He's the heir.'

20:15 "They threw him out of the vineyard
And then killed the owner's son.
Now the owner of the vineyard,
To them what will he have done?

20:16 "He'll come and destroy these farmers.
To others the vineyard he'll grant."
And when the crowd heard this, they said,
"To happen, this just can't!"

20:17 But Jesus looked at them and said,
"What's written, have you not known,
'That rock the builders rejected
Became the chief cornerstone'?

20:18 "Everyone who falls on that stone
Will most certainly shatter,
But on whomever that stone falls,
Him, like dust, it will scatter."

20:19 That same hour the chief priests and scribes
Tried to take Jesus by force,
But fearing the crowd around Him,
They desisted from this course.[133]

For they all knew that against them
The parable Jesus told.
20:20 Therefore, they watched Him very close
So of Him they could take hold.

Spies pretending to be righteous,
They sent to hear Jesus preach,
So by His words they could trap Him,
And with them they could impeach.*

This way they would have solid grounds
For Jesus's captivity
And give Him to the governor's
Power and authority.

20:21 They questioned Him saying, "Teacher,
We all know in what You say
That You correctly speak and teach,
And favorites You do not play.

"You teach the way of God in truth.
So what answer have You got?*
20:22 As for paying Caesar taxes,
Is this lawful for us or not?"

20:23 But seeing through their trickery,
20:24 He answered, "To Me please show
A coin called a denarius
So this answer you may know.*

"Whose image and whose inscription
Does this denarius bear?"
They answered back, "It is Caesar's."
20:25 He said, "The answer is right there.*

"You then must render to Caesar
So that you won't be at odds.*
Pay to Caesar what is Caesar's,
And to God pay what is God's."

20:26 They grew silent by His answer,
Amazed by what they had heard.
In public they were unable
To trap Him in any word.

20:27 Now some Sadducees approached Him,
And to Him posed this question.
(The Sadducees are those who say
There is no resurrection.)

20:28 "O Teacher, Moses wrote for us,
That if a man's brother dies,
Leaving a wife but no children,
That the brother must arise.

"He must go to his brother's wife
And take her to be his mate,[134]
And on behalf of his brother
Descendants he must create.

20:29 "Suppose there were seven brothers,
And the oldest took a bride.
They did not have any children
When the oldest brother died.

20:30 "Now the second brother took her,
But no offspring did they see.
He died leaving her childless too,
20:31 And so also brother three.

"In fact, all seven brothers died,
Unable to procreate.
20:32 Finally the woman also died.
This puzzle we now relate.*

20:33 "Since all seven had married her,
This creates one big question:*
Which one's wife will she then become
In the resurrection?"

20:34 To them Jesus gave this answer:
"All the people of this age
Are made up of males and females,[135]
And so in marriage engage.

20:35 "But those deemed worthy to attain
Resurrection from the dead,
In that future age they will live,
But not one of them will wed.[136]

20:36 "For they cannot die anymore.
Like angels they have perfection,
For they are both the sons of God
And of the resurrection.

20:37 "To show that the dead are raised up,
Even Moses made this clear.
It's in the account of the bush
Where the Lord God did appear.*

"He tells what the Lord called Himself,
The God of the following men:
Abraham, Isaac, and Jacob,
Who had already died by then.*

20:38 "God is not the God of the dead.
These three men He will revive,[137]
But He's the God of the living.
So to Him they're all alive."

20:39 Now some of the scribes answered back,
"Teacher, You have well declared."
20:40 So to ask Him any questions,
Not one of them even dared.

20:41 So He asked them, "How is it true
That they call Christ David's son?
20:42 David writes in the book of Psalms
About the Anointed One.*

"He writes, 'The LORD said to My Lord:
At My right hand take Your seat
20:43 *Until I make Your enemies*
A footstool under Your feet.'

20:44 "David, therefore, calls the Christ, 'Lord,'
The Christ who was yet to come.*
Because he calls the Christ his Lord,
How then can He be his son?"

20:45 While the whole crowd was listening,
To the disciples He said,
20:46 "I tell you watch out for the scribes
Who wish in long robes to tread.

"Beware of those who love salutes
Given in the market streets,
Who at the synagogues love to sit
In the most important seats.

"Beware of those who at the feasts
Love to sit in honored chairs,
20:47 Who devour houses of widows,
Who for show offer long prayers.

"Beware of the scribes who pursue*
This kind of aspiration,*
For they will certainly receive
The greater condemnation."

21:1 Jesus then looked up and noticed
How certain people would pitch
Money into the treasury.
Those people were very rich.

21:2 But then he noticed a widow
Who lived in deep poverty
Drop her last two small copper coins
Right into the treasury.

21:3 So He said, "I tell you the truth,
This widow who's now deprived
Has given more than all of them
Who in abundance have thrived.*

21:4 "Because out of their abundance
They gave to the treasury,
But she gave everything she had,
Giving from her poverty."

21:5 Now some people were conversing
(For they were very impressed)*
How with gifts and beautiful stones
Herod's[138] temple had been dressed.

21:6 So Jesus said, "These things you see
Will all be torn down one day,
Not one stone left on another.
In ruins these things will lay."

21:7 They questioned Him, saying, "Teacher!
When will all these things take place?
What sign should we be looking for
In this particular case?"

21:8 "Keep on the alert," Jesus said,
"That deceived you will not be,
For many will come in My name,
Proclaiming themselves as Me.

"They will proclaim, 'I am the One,'
And will say, 'The time is near,'
But do not follow after them.
Don't even give them your ear.*

21:9 "When you hear of wars and revolts,
Your own fears you must combat,
For all those things must happen first,
But the end won't follow that.

21:10 "Nation will rise against nation,"
Jesus continued to state,
"Kingdoms will rise against kingdoms,
21:11 And the earthquakes will be great.

"Plagues and famines will too occur
In places of many kinds,
And from heaven terrors will come
As well as tremendous signs.

21:12 "But before these events occur
On account of My name's sake,
They will lay their hands upon you.
Trouble for you they will make.*

"You they'll pursue and persecute.
You to all these they will take:
Synagogues, jails, kings, and rulers,
On account of My name's sake.

21:13 "Thus, you'll have opportunity
Your testimony to share,
21:14 But in your hearts ahead of time
Your defense do not prepare.

21:15 "For I Myself will give to you
A message that is astute,
Which none of your opponents can
Resist or even refute.

21:16 "And you will be delivered up
By your fathers and mothers,
By your friends and your relatives,
And by your fellow brothers.

"Some of you will be put to death.
21:17 And since My name you cherish,
21:18 All will hate you, yet not one hair
From your head will perish.

21:19 "By endurance you'll gain your lives,
21:20 And when you see these appear,
Armies circling Jerusalem,
Know her destruction is near.

21:21 "Then let the ones in Judea
Up into the mountains race.
As for those within the city,
Let them also leave that place.

"Don't let the ones in the country
Enter the city, not one.
21:22 For to fulfill all that's written,
The days of vengeance have come.

21:23 "Pregnant women and those who nurse,
Woe to them all in that day.
On this land great distress will come.
On this people wrath will weigh.

21:24 "By the edge of the sword they'll fall,
And the rest who do withstand,*
They'll be taken as prisoners
Into every Gentile land.

"By the Gentiles, Jerusalem
Will be trampled in defeat.
This will continue 'til the times
Of the Gentiles are complete.

21:25 "There'll be signs in sun, moon, and stars.
On earth, nations' fears will soar
As in despair they watch the sea
And waves continue to roar.

21:26 "There'll be people fainting from fear,
This while they anticipate
The things coming upon the world
As the heavens agitate.

21:27 "Then they'll see coming in a cloud
The Son of Man with power,
And with great glory He will come
In that unforeseen hour.

21:28 "Stand when these things start to take place.
Lift up your heads without fear
Because your final redemption
Is then drawing very near."

21:29 Then He told them a parable
In order to illustrate:*
"Note the fig trees and all the trees
21:30 And the signs they do relate.

"As soon as they begin to bud,
You all know from what you see
That the summer is close at hand.
It is nearing rapidly.*

21:31 "So also when you see these signs,
Those in the heavenly sky,[139]
Realize that the kingdom of God
Is then drawing very nigh.

21:32 “Concerning this generation,
I’m telling the truth to you,
It will by no means pass away
Until all the things come true.

21:33 “This very earth will pass away,
Also the celestial sky,
But My words will not pass away.
In no way will My words die.*

21:34 “Keep guarding yourselves that your hearts
Won’t be weighed down by excess,
Not by the worries of this life,
And neither by drunkenness.

“Keep guarding yourselves so that day
Won’t come on you like a snare,
21:35 For all who sit on the earth’s face,
It will catch them unaware.

21:36 “Keep staying alert at all times
By praying before God’s face
So you may have strength to escape
All that’s about to take place.

“Keep staying alert at all times
With prayer being your plan
So that you may be able to
Stand before the Son of Man.”

21:37 He was teaching in the temple
Only in the daylight time,
For at evening He would go out.
Mount Olivet He would climb.

On the mount He would spend the night,
21:38 And all the people would come
To the temple to hear Him speak
At the rising of the sun.[140]

22:1 Now the time of the festival,
The Feast of Unleavened Bread,
Also known as the Passover,
Was approaching just ahead.

22:2 And so the chief priest and the scribes
Were trying to figure ways
How they might put Jesus to death,
For they feared the crowd those days.

22:3 Then Satan went into Judas
(Iscariot, *that is to say,
Who had been numbered with the Twelve).
22:4 Therefore, Judas went away.

To the chief priests and officers
Judas went and then conferred
How to betray Jesus to them,
22:5 And they rejoiced at his word.

They arranged to give him money.
22:6 He agreed and then reviewed
The best time to betray Jesus
Apart from the multitude.

22:7 The first day of Unleavened Bread
Then arrived to be fulfilled,
The day on which the Passover
Was required to be killed.

22:8 Then Jesus sent Peter and John
To carry out His request:
"Go prepare us the Passover
So that it we may ingest."

22:9 To Him they asked, "Where do You wish
For us to prepare this meal?"
22:10 He said to them, "Take careful note,
The details I now reveal.*

"After you enter the city,
A certain man you will meet.
He'll be bearing a water jug.
Go follow after his feet.

"Whatever house he enters in,
That house you enter as well,
22:11 And to the owner of the house
This message you then must tell:

"'The Teacher asks you, *Where's the room,*
The guest room in which to dine
Where I may eat the Passover
With the disciples of Mine?'

22:12 "He will show you an upper room
All furnished and with much space,
And you will then prepare the meal
Right there in that very place."

22:13 So then the two went on their way,
And all that Jesus declared
They found to be just as He said.
The Passover they prepared.

22:14 And when the hour had arrived,
At the table He reclined.
The apostles He had chosen
Along with Him also dined.

22:15 He said to them, "This Passover
I have earnestly desired
To eat with you before the time
I suffer, *as is required.

22:16 "For now I say to all of you,
This meal I will never eat
Until the time in God's kingdom
Has at last been made complete."

22:17 Jesus took a drinking vessel
While giving thanks for the cup.
He said to them, "Among yourselves
Take this and divide it up.

22:18 "For not until God's kingdom comes,
Beginning now, at this time,
I tell you I won't drink this fruit
Which is produced from the vine."

22:19 Then Jesus took one of the loaves
While giving thanks for the bread.
He broke it and distributed it
As to them these words He said:

"This is My body given up
On your behalf, in your stead.
You all are to remember Me
Whenever you eat this bread."

22:20 In the same way, He took the cup
After they'd eaten and said,
"This cup is the new covenant,
My blood poured out in your stead."

22:21 "Nevertheless, at this table
With Me is one who'll betray.
The hand who will deliver Me,
Behold, take notice, I say!

22:22 "For while it's true the Son of Man
Is on His way as decreed,
The man by whom He is betrayed,
Horror to that man, indeed."

22:23 They started talking back and forth
As to whom would do such a deed.
Who was going to do this thing
That Jesus had just decreed?

22:24 In the course of their discussion
A great dispute did befall
As to which one was considered
The greatest one of them all.

22:25 He said to them, "The pagan kings,
Their lordship they do assert.
'Benefactors' these kings are called
For the power they exert.

22:26 "Nevertheless, among yourselves,
This is not how it's to be done.
Let him who thinks he's the greater
Take the role of the younger one.

"Let him who thinks he's the leader
Become a servant to all.
You've overlooked the obvious*
In the course of your verbal brawl.*

22:27 "For who's greater, the one who sits
Or the one who serves the food?
Is it not the person who sits?
But how am I to be viewed?*

"I'm among you as one who serves,
And you are the ones who sit.*
Let him who thinks he's the leader*
To servanthood then commit.*

22:28 "You've stayed with Me in My trials.
22:29 So a kingdom I assign.
I confer to you this kingdom
As My Father gave Me Mine.

22:30 "For this reason I give to you
That in this kingdom of Mine
You all may eat at My table.
You all may drink as you dine.

"And upon thrones you all will sit,
And judgment you will convey
On the twelve tribes of Israel
In the kingdom of that day.*

22:31 "Simon, Simon, listen to Me.
Evil Satan did entreat.
He's petitioned God to allow
You to be sifted like wheat.

22:32 "But so that your faith may not fail,
I have prayed for you at length,
And when you have turned back again,
You must give your brothers strength."

22:33 But Peter said to Jesus, "Lord!
My faithfulness, it is true.
I'm ready to go to prison
And even to die with You."

22:34 "I tell you Peter," Jesus said,
"This day the cock will not crow
Until you have denied three times
That Me you do even know."

22:35 He asked them, "When I sent you out
With no sandals, purse, or sack,
Did you ever need anything?"
They said, "No, we did not lack!"

22:36 He said to them, "But at this time,
This strategy now suppose:*
Let him who owns a money purse
Take it wherever he goes.

"Likewise let him who owns a sack
Take it wherever he goes,
And let the one who has no sword
Get one by selling his clothes.

22:37 "For in Me the words must come true
That about Me has been penned.
'He was numbered with transgressors'
Is about to see its end."

22:38 And they said to Him, "Look! O Lord,
We have these swords, only two."
Then Jesus replied back to them,
"Those two swords, they will do."

22:39 Then Jesus went out from the house,
And in His usual way
Journeyed to the Mount of Olives,
The place where He'd stop and pray.*

His disciples traveled with Him,
22:40 And arriving at that place,
He said, "Keep praying so you won't
Fall into temptation's face."

22:41 From the disciples He withdrew
About a stone's throw away,
Where He knelt down upon His knees,
And these words began to pray:

22:42 "Father, if you determine it,
This cup from My hand, please take,
Yet let not My own will be done.
Let all things be for Your sake."

22:43 There came an angel from heaven,
Who before Jesus appeared.
The angel came to strengthen Him.
The Lord Jesus persevered.*

22:44 He was praying so fervently
As agony did abound.
As drops of blood His sweat became
That fell down upon the ground.[141]

22:45 When from His praying He arose,
To His disciples He went.
He found them sleeping due to grief,
To sorrow of great extent.*

22:46 He said to them, "Now tell Me why
You are sleeping in this case.
Get up and pray so you will not
Fall into temptation's face."

22:47 While He was still speaking to them,
Behold, a multitude came.
One of the Twelve was leading them,
And Judas was that one's name.

He approached Jesus to kiss Him,
22:48 But Jesus to him said this,
"O Judas, are you betraying
The Son of Man with a kiss?"

22:49 Then the ones with Him did realize
What was happening to the Lord.
They asked Him, "Master, is it time
To strike, to take up the sword?"

22:50 Now one of the disciples there
To the multitude drew near.*
He swung and struck the high priest's slave,
Severing the slave's right ear.

22:51 Jesus responded, saying, "Stop!
Stop your swinging with the sword."
Then Jesus touched the wounded ear.
The ear was fully restored.

22:52 To the chief priests and the elders,
To the temple officers,
To all those coming against Him,
He confronted with these words:

"Have you come out with swords and clubs
As if a robber to seek?
22:53 At the temple I was with you
Every single day this week.

"Yet you did not lay hands on Me.
Yes, from this you did refrain,*
But now the time belongs to you
When the darkness does now reign."

22:54 Then after taking hold of Him,
They led Jesus from that place,
Brought Him into the high priest's house
Who questioned Him face to face.[142]

Now following them was Peter,
But a distance from their sight.
22:55 In the middle of the courtyard
A nice warm fire they did light.

They all sat down together there
As Jesus was on trial,*
And Peter slipped into their midst,
Sitting there all the while.

22:56 Now a certain slave girl saw him
As he sat in the firelight.
She said, looking closely at him,
"This one was with Him, all right!"

22:57 But Peter quickly reacted*
By giving her this reply,
"Woman, I don't know who He is!"
Her charge Peter did deny.

22:58 Shortly after, another said,
When Peter, this one did spot,
"You are certainly one of them!"
But Peter said, "Man, I'm not!"

22:59 After about one hour had passed,
Another man did demand,
"This one's a Galilean too.
Yes, he was part of His band."

22:60 But Peter replied, "What you say,
Man, I tell you, I don't know!"
And as he spoke those very words,
A rooster right then did crow.

22:61 Then the Lord turned and looked at him.
All His words, Peter recalled,
"Before it crows, You'll deny Me thrice."
22:62 Then Peter went out and bawled.

22:63 The men who were guarding Jesus,
They began to scorn and mock,
And they were also beating Him,
Taunting Him with all their talk.*

22:64 Blindfolding Him, they were asking,
"Who hit you? Now prophesy!"
22:65 They said much more things against Him.
Great blasphemies they did cry.

22:66 The elders of the people met
Just as soon as it was day.
This included chief priests and scribes,
And they led Jesus away.

They brought Him to their council room.
Many questions they then fired.
22:67 "If You're the Christ, confess this now,"
His answer they all required.*

But Jesus said, "If I tell you,
In no way will you believe,
22:68 And if I ask you a question,
An answer I won't receive.

22:69 "But from now on, the Son of Man
Will be seated in this place,
At the right hand of God's power,"
Jesus spoke before their face.*

22:70 "So then are You the Son of God?"
They continued the exam.
He replied, "What you are asking,
That's exactly who I am."

22:71 They said, "What further need is there
For testimony to hear?
For what we've heard from His own mouth
Is unmistakably clear."[143]

23:1 Then all of them assembled there
Got up and brought Jesus out.
They led Him away to Pilate,
23:2 And these charges they did spout:

"We found Him tricking our nation.
So to you this man we bring.*
He forbids to pay Caesar dues.
He claims to be Christ, a king."

23:3 "So are you the King of the Jews?"
Pilate began to survey.
Jesus then answered him and said,
"It is so, just as you say."

23:4 To the chief priests and to the crowds
Pilate gave his summation,
"In this man I find no basis
For any accusation."

23:5 "But He stirs people everywhere,"
They insisted with their case,
"Teaching all over Judea,
From Galilee to this place."

23:6 As soon as Pilate heard these words,
Right away he sought to know
If this Man was from Galilee,
And he asked if it was so.

23:7 When he learned that Jesus belonged
To Herod's jurisdiction,
He sent Him so that Herod would
Determine a conviction.*

Herod was in Jerusalem
As it so happened to be.
When he saw Jesus, he was glad,
For Him he had longed to see.

23:8 Because of all that he had heard,
He had this wish for some time,
Hoping to see Jesus perform
Just one miraculous sign.

23:9 Herod questioned Him at great length,
Yet Jesus gave no reply,
23:10 While with hurling accusations,
The chief priests and scribes stood by.

23:11 After treating Him with contempt
And mocking Him to excess,
Herod with his army of men
Put Jesus in splendid dress.

Herod sent Him back to Pilate,
Dressed in this elegant way.
23:12 Herod and Pilate were at odds,
But became good friends that day.

23:13 Then the chief priests, Pilate summoned,
And all the rulers as well,
And he summoned all the people,
Not one group did he dispel.*

23:14 He said to all those assembled,
"This Man to me you have brought
With charges of stirring people
For some rebellious plot.

"Behold, I have examined Him
In the presence of your face,
Yet in this Man I find no guilt
In the charges of your case.

23:15 "Not even Herod sees your charge,
For he sent us back this One.
Behold, nothing deserving death
By Jesus has yet been done.

23:16 "I will therefore just punish Him,
And Him I then will let go."[144]
23:18 But they cried out altogether,
"Don't release Jesus! Oh no!

"Release for us Barabbas now,
And take this Man we have brought!"
23:19 (Now Barabbas was imprisoned
For a seditious plot.

In that city he was behind
A certain plot to rebel.
For that crime he was imprisoned,
Also for murder as well.)

23:20 Now wishing to set Jesus free,
Pilate made another try,
23:21 But they kept shouting all the more,
"Crucify Him, crucify!"

23:22 The third time Pilate said to them,
"What evil has Jesus done?
There is no cause to have Him killed.
I've found no guilt in this One.

"Since He has not done anything
For death to be the decree,
I will just simply punish Him,
And then I will set Him free."

23:23 But they were being insistent,
Demanding with voices great
That Jesus should be crucified,
And their cries did dominate.

23:24 So final judgment Pilate passed,
Granting them their petition.
23:25 He released the man imprisoned
For murder and sedition.

Then he handed Jesus over
To the gathered people's will.
They took Jesus, led Him away,
For Him they wanted to kill.*

23:26 On the way, Simon of Cyrene,
Who from the country had come,
Was grabbed and forced to bear the cross,
Following behind God's Son.[145]

23:27 There was a very large number
Of people trailing behind,
Also great numbers of women
Who over Him wailed and whined.

23:28 "Now stop your weeping over Me,"
Jesus turned and said to them.
"Weep for yourselves and your children,
Daughters of Jerusalem.

23:29 "For days are coming when they'll say,
'The barren ones are not cursed.[146]
Blessed are the wombs that never bore
And the breasts that never nursed.'

23:30 "Then they will say to the mountains,
'Fall on us!' *wishing to die.
They also will turn to the hills.
'Cover us!' they all will cry.

23:31 "For although when the wood is green,
These practices they apply,
What will most certainly happen
When the wood is seasoned dry?"

23:32 Now there also were two others
Who were to be killed that day.
So with Jesus these criminals
Were also being led away.

23:33 They came to the place of The Skull,
Of the crucifixion site.
One was crucified to Christ's left,
The other one to His right.

23:34 But praying out loud, Jesus said,
"O Father, forgive them please,
For they don't know what they're doing."
Now His clothing they did seize.

They divided up the clothing.
The soldiers did this, unfazed,[147]
By casting lots for every piece
23:35 As the people stood by and gazed.

Even the rulers scoffed at Him.
"He has saved others," they said.
"If He's God's Christ, God's Chosen One,
Then let Him save His own head."

23:36 The soldiers also scoffed at Him
As they offered Him sour wine,
23:37 Saying, "If You're King of the Jews,
Then save Yourself at this time!"

23:38 The crime for which He was accused*
Was put on a sign, which read,
"This one is the King of the Jews,"
And it hung above His head.

23:39 One criminal, while hanging there,
Insults at Jesus did spew,
"Are You the Christ, or are You not?
Save Yourself and save us too!"

23:40 But the other one rebuked him,
Revealing his repentance,*
"Do you possess no fear of God?
You're under the same sentence!

23:41 "For justly we have been condemned,
And deserving all along
What we're receiving for our deeds,
But this Man has done no wrong."

23:42 And this criminal also said,
Giving to Jesus this plea:
"When You come into Your kingdom,
Jesus, please remember me!"

23:43 Jesus responded back to him,
"This truth to you I decree,
This very day in Paradise
You will truly be with Me!"

23:44 Now it was about the sixth hour
When the sun refused to shine.
Darkness engulfed the entire land
For a three-hour span of time.[148]

23:45 The temple veil was torn in two,
And then about three o'clock,[149]
23:46 In a loud voice to the Father
He began to plainly talk.

"In Your hands I give My spirit,
O My Father," Jesus cried.
After saying these very words,
He breathed His last and then died.

23:47 When the centurion saw this,
To God he then gave praise,
"This Man was truly innocent
And righteous in all His ways."

23:48 The various crowds gathered there
To observe all the disgrace
Returned back home, beating their breasts
After seeing what took place.

23:49 All the men who knew Jesus well,
Along with the female crew
Who followed Him from Galilee
Stood afar seeing this too.

23:50 Later a man named Joseph came,
Both a good and righteous man.
To the Sanhedrin he belonged,
23:51 But he had opposed their plan.

Arimathea he was from,
A city that had all Jews.
He was waiting for God's kingdom,
Expectant of the good news.*

23:52 Now this man had gone to Pilate
To make a respectful plea.[150]
For Jesus's body he did ask,
To which Pilate did agree.[151]

23:53 So Joseph came and took it down.
Care to the body he gave.
He wrapped it in a linen cloth
And laid Jesus in a grave.

The grave was carved into a rock
Where nobody had ever been.
23:54 Now it was preparation day,
But the Sabbath was to begin.

23:55 The women, who from Galilee
Had followed Jesus and stayed,
Followed Joseph and saw the tomb
And how His body was laid.

23:56 They prepared spices and perfumes,
Leaving the site of the grave,
Then rested on the Sabbath day,
Obeying the command God gave.

24:1 Then on the first day of the week
As it was becoming light,
With the spices they had prepared
They arrived back at the site.

24:2 They found that the stone to the tomb
Had been rolled away from there.
24:3 They entered in but could not find
The Lord's[152] body anywhere.

24:4 Concerning this they were perplexed,
And as they were in dismay,
Behold, before them two men stood
In spectacular array.

24:5 In their terror the women bowed
Their faces down to the floor,
But the men asked, "Why do you seek
The One who is dead no more?

"Why do you seek the Living One
Among the ones who are dead?
24:6 He's not here, but He has risen.
Now remember what He said.

"Remember what He spoke to you
While with you in Galilee.
24:7 He told you what was to take place
Out of great necessity.

"He told you that the Son of Man
Must be delivered up first
Into the hands of sinful men
And then become the cursed.*

"He told you that the Son of Man
Must then become crucified
But then would rise up from the dead
The third day after He died."

24:8 Then they remembered Jesus's words.
24:9 So from the tomb they returned.
To the Eleven and the rest
They told all they had learned.

24:10 Now among this group of women,
Who told what they all had seen,
Were Mary of James, Joanna,
And Mary Magdalene.

They were telling the apostles
Everything that they had heard,
24:11 But they refused to believe them
Since it all seemed too absurd.

24:12 Peter got up, ran to the tomb,
And then stooped down to inspect.
The linen clothes for burial
Was all that he could detect.

Then walking away from the tomb,
To wonder Peter resigned.
What exactly might have happened
He just pondered in his mind.

24:13 Behold, two of the disciples
Were going that very day
From Jerusalem to Emmaus,
Which was seven miles away.

24:14 They were talking with each other
Of the things that came about,
24:15 And during their conversation,
Jesus joined them on their route.

24:16 But their eyes were being restrained
So that Him they did not know.
24:17 He said to them, "What are these words
You're discussing while you go?"

At this question, with faces sad,
They stopped from moving ahead.
24:18 Now one of them, named Cleopas,
Responded to Him and said:

"Of Jerusalem's visitors,
Are You just the only one
Who does not know that in these days
All the things that have been done?"

24:19 "What things?" Jesus said back to them,
To which the two then replied,
"About Jesus of Nazareth,
The One who was crucified.[153]

"A prophet this Man truly was.
With power He did excel
In word and deed before God's eyes
And everyone's eyes as well.

24:20 "But the chief priests and our rulers
Gave Him over to be tried
So that to death He'd be sentenced,
And then Him they crucified.

24:21 "Now we were very much hoping
That Jesus Himself would be
The One who was supposed to come
To set all Israel free.

"However, besides all of this,
The third day has already come
Since the time all these things occurred,
When all these events were done.*

24:22 "But very early this morning
Some women were at His grave.
These women belonged to our group.
An awesome report they gave.

24:23 "They did not find His body there
And came back to us and said
They'd seen a vision of angels,
Saying He's alive, not dead.

24:24 "Then certain men who were with us
Went out to the tomb and found
Everything as the women said,
But Jesus was not around."

24:25 Then Jesus said to these two men,
"How foolish to be broken.[154]
You are slow in heart to believe
All that the prophets have spoken.

24:26 "Was it not of necessity
For Christ to suffer this way
And then to enter His glory
Just as the prophets did say?"

24:27 So then beginning with Moses
And with all the Prophets next,
He explained all about Himself
That was in the sacred text.

24:28 As they came near to the village
Of their final destination,
He acted as if time with them
Had reached its culmination.

24:29 They urged Him, saying, "Stay with us,
For evening is almost here.
The day has now drawn to a close,
And our place is very near."*

So He went in to stay with them,
24:30 And later when it was time,
He then reclined at the table
In order with them to dine.

Then taking the bread He blessed it
And broke it and gave it out.
And as He did this with the bread,
24:31 Who He was they had no doubt.

For then their eyes were opened up.
All their gloom turned to delight,*
But when they realized who He was,
He disappeared from their sight.

24:32 Then the two said to each other,
But this time in retrospect,*
"When He spoke to us on the road,
Remember all the effect.

"While to us He was explaining
The Scriptures so we could learn
How the Christ fulfilled prophecy,*
Did not our own hearts just burn?"

24:33 Right then back to Jerusalem
They returned to their brothers.[155]
They found the Eleven gathered,
And with them many others.

24:34 The congregation told the two,
"The Lord has risen indeed,
For to Simon He has appeared.
He's risen as He decreed!"*

24:35 The two disciples then explained
How on their journey He spoke
And how they recognized the Lord
When the loaf of bread He broke.

24:36 As they talked, He stood before them,
"Peace to you all!" Jesus said.
24:37 Thinking that He was a spirit,
They were scared and full of dread.

24:38 "Why be troubled?" He said to them,
"In your hearts why let doubts rise?
24:39 Here are My hands, also My feet.
Look here and now analyze.

"Observe that it is I Myself.
Go ahead touch Me as well.
A spirit has not flesh and bones,
But I do as you can tell."

24:40 As He was saying all of this,
He showed them His hands and feet.
24:41 Shocked with joy, they did not believe.
So He asked, "What's here to eat?"

24:42 They gave Him a piece of broiled fish,
24:43 Which He ate before their eyes.
24:44 "These are My words I spoke to you,"
He began to summarize.

"All that is written about Me,
I told you while with you still.
In the Law,[156] the Prophets, and Psalms,
All this I had to fulfill."

24:45 So to understand the Scriptures,
Jesus opened up each mind.
24:46 "In the writings," He said to them,
"All these things are what we find:

"Christ must suffer. Then from the dead
He must rise on the third day.
24:47 Repentance for forgiveness of sins
Must be announced this way:

"In His name to every nation
(No nation is to be spared),*
Beginning from Jerusalem,
This message must now be shared.

24:48 "You are witnesses of these things,
24:49 But take note of what I'll do.
I am sending out the promise
Of My Father upon you.

"But you must stay in this city
Until that one great event*
When you clothe yourselves with power
That from on high will be sent."

24:50 He led them out near Bethany,
And blessed them with His hands raised.
24:51 During this He went to heaven,
24:52 And they worshipped Him and praised.

To Jerusalem they returned
With gladness unabated.
24:53 They kept meeting in the temple,
Praising God as they waited.

THE POETIC BOOK OF ACTS

1:1 The first account, Theophilus,
That I had compiled with facts
Covered all that Jesus began,
Both His teachings and His acts.

1:2 It covered up until the day
He went up into heaven,
After He had by God's Spirit
Commanded His Eleven.*

All these men were His apostles
Whom He Himself selected,
1:3 To whom also He showed Himself
As being resurrected.

He resurrected from the dead
After suffering a lot
And gave many convincing proofs
That deceased He was not.

Jesus appeared at various times
Over a forty-day span,
Speaking to them of God's kingdom,
Explaining to them God's plan.*

1:4 One time while gathered together,
Jesus told them not to leave,
But to wait in Jerusalem
For the Spirit to receive.

This the Father had promised them,
About whom Jesus had taught,
"Of this One you have heard from Me
That the Father would allot.

1:5 "For John baptized you in water,
But in a few days, that's when,
In the Holy Spirit of God,
You all will be baptized then."

1:6 While together they were asking,
"Is this now the time, O Lord,
That the kingdom to Israel
By You will become restored?"

1:7 He said to them, "You're not to know
The seasons or the dates
That have been set by the Father
As His own power dictates.

1:8 "But you'll receive certain power,
Each one of you in this squad,*
When upon you the Spirit comes,
The Holy Spirit of God.

"And you will be My witnesses.
In Jerusalem, you will start,
All Judea, Samaria,
And then to the world's last part."

1:9 After saying all of these things,
He was lifted to the skies.
As they watched Him, a cloud then came
And removed Him from their eyes.

1:10 After seeing Him go away,
They just stared into the sky.
Then suddenly there were two men
In white clothing standing by.

1:11 They said to those looking up high,
"O you men of Galilee,
Why keep staring into the sky?
Why keep standing inactively?

"This same Jesus taken from you
Up into heaven, O men,
In the same way you watched Him go,
In that way He'll come again."

1:12 Then they returned from Olivet,
The mountain, *that is to say,
Which was nearby Jerusalem,
A Sabbath's day walk away.

They returned to Jerusalem,
1:13 And when arriving there,
The upper room of where they stayed,
They entered in for prayer.

The men to whom I'm referring
Are apostles with these names:[157]
There was Peter, known as Cephas,
John, and his brother, James.

There was Andrew, Phillip, and Simon,
The Zealot, as he was known.
There was Thomas, who believed not
'Til Christ's wounds to him were shown.

There was James, the son of Alpheus,
And Matthew, an outcast Jew.
There was Judas, the son of James,
And also Bartholomew.

1:14 All of these men in one accord
Continued on in prayer,
But not only the apostles,
Others were also there.

There was Mary, Jesus's mother,
There were other women too;
There were also Jesus's brothers,
Just to single out a few.*

1:15 Now in those days Peter stood up
Among his fellow men.
The crowd numbered approximately
One hundred twenty then.

1:16 "Men and brothers," Peter addressed,
"The Scripture, which was willed
By the Spirit[158] through David's mouth,
It had to be fulfilled.

"The Spirit spoke about Judas,
Who was a guide to these,
To the mob who came to Jesus
To arrest Him and to seize.

1:17 "Judas was one of our number,
And was chosen to take part
In this service, this ministry,
But was wicked in his heart."*

1:18 (This man, therefore, bought for himself
From the wages that he got
For his wicked and evil deed
A piece of land, a plot.

Falling facedown upon this plot,
His middle burst open wide.
From his belly there then gushed out
Everything that was inside.

1:19 And all throughout Jerusalem
This story spread like a flood.
"Hakeldama," they called the field,
Or in Greek, "The Field of Blood.")

1:20 "For it reads in the book of Psalms,"
Peter continued to tell,[159]
"'Let his homestead be deserted.
In it let no person dwell.'

"Also in Psalms it's been written,
But another place it's stressed,[160]
'Let someone else, another man,
Take the office he possessed.'

1:21 "Therefore, out of necessity,
We must now select a man
Who has been with us from the time
The Lord Jesus's work began.

1:22 "It started with John's baptism
And continued 'til the day
Jesus was snatched from our presence
And to heaven went away.

"The Lord went in and out from us,
And one of those who were there,
Concerning His resurrection,
Should now in our witness share."

1:23 And so they chose two candidates,
Joseph and Matthias.
(Joseph was Barsabbas or Justus.)
They then removed all bias.*

1:24 They prayed, "O Lord, who knows all hearts,
Show us which one of these two
Should occupy this ministry.
Which one is chosen by You?

1:25 "This service and apostleship,
From which Judas turned aside
To go to the place he belonged,
Must now become occupied."

1:26 So they drew lots between the two,
And the lot fell to Matthias.
With the eleven apostles
He was numbered without bias.[161]

2:1 Now when the day of Pentecost
Had not yet fully past,
They were gathered together still
In the same place as the last.

2:2 Then suddenly from heaven came
A sound like a violent wind.
It filled the house where they were at
Throughout from end to end.

2:3 Then they saw tongues that looked like fire,
Splitting and moving around,
Coming to rest on each of them
2:4 As words they began to sound.

With the Holy Spirit of God
They all were completely filled.
The words were other languages
That the Spirit had instilled.

2:5 Jerusalem was filled with Jews,
With devout men staying there
From each nation under heaven.
These Jews were everywhere.*

2:6 The Jewish crowd came together
When this mighty sound occurred.
They were confused and mystified
By all that they had heard.

Each one of them could understand
The message being declared,
For it was in their dialect
That the disciples had shared.

2:7 They were amazed and marveled much
And then proceeded to say,
"Are not they all Galileans?
Just how can they speak this way?

2:8 "How can it be that we each hear
In our own dialect
The tongue in which we each were born,
Unknown to this Jewish sect?[162]

2:9 "The dialects of Parthians,
Of Elamites and of Medes,
Of those from Mesopatamia,
And those of Judean breeds.

"Asian and Pontus dialects,
Cappadocia as well,
2:10 Phrygia and Pamphylia,
And those who in Egypt dwell.

"The dialects of those who live
In Libya near Cyrene,
Of proselytes and Jews from Rome,
Visiting at this scene.

2:11 "The dialects of the Cretans
And of the Arabs too.
We hear them speak of God's great deeds
In our own tongues—we do!"

2:12 They continued in amazement
Yet were also mystified.
They were saying to each other,
"What meaning must be applied?"

2:13 But some others just sneered and mocked
With language that was malign.
This conclusion some verbalized,
"They're drunk. They're full of sweet wine."

2:14 But Peter with the Eleven
Stood up to address the crowd.
"Men of Judea," he began
In a voice extremely loud.

"To all who live in Jerusalem,
To you all, let this be clear,
To all the words that I now say,
Pay heed! Give me your ear!

2:15 "These can't be drunk as you suppose.
It's the third hour of the day.
2:16 What you have heard, the prophet Joel
From the Lord has this to say:

2:17 "'It will occur in the last days
That My Spirit I'll pour out
To fall upon all of mankind.
This will surely come about.*

"'Sons and daughters will prophesy
From future generations.
Your youthful men will see visions.
Elders will dream revelations.

2:18 "'On My bond slaves I will pour out
My own Spirit in those days.
Men and women will prophesy
As the Spirit sets them ablaze.[163]

2:19 "'And wonders in the sky above
And signs on the earth below,
Blood, fire, and vapor of smoke,
I'll assuredly bestow.

2:20 "'Into darkness the sun will turn,
The moon—a blood-filled mass
Before that great and glorious day
Of the Lord should come to pass.

2:21 "'And it shall be that in that day
Everyone, regardless* of race,
Who calls on the name of the Lord
Will be saved *by the Lord's grace.'

2:22 "Hear these words, men of Israel:
Jesus the Nazarene—
A man proven to you by God
Through mighty works you have seen—

"With signs, wonders, and miracles
God worked through Him as you know,
For in your midst He did these things,
2:23 Yet death He did not forgo.

"For by God's plan and foreknowledge,
That which He had long ordained,
This Jesus was delivered up
In order to be arraigned.*

"By the hand of ungodly men
You raised Him up to the sky,
Nailing Him to a wooden cross.
Him you did crucify.

2:24 "But breaking loose the bonds of death,
God raised Him up from the dead
Since by its grip He can't be held,
2:25 Which is just as David said:

"'I was always seeing the Lord
Before my very own face,
For He is there at my right hand
So I won't be moved out of place.

2:26 "'Because of this, my heart is cheered.
With joy my tongue is supplied.
Even my body, based on hope,
Will continue to abide.

2:27 "'For You will not desert my soul
In Hades for it to stay,
Nor will You let Your Holy One
Undergo any decay.

2:28 "'For all the ways that lead to life,
You have made these known to me.
You will make me full of gladness
When You, face to face I see.'

2:29 "Brothers, the patriarch David,
Of him I can boldly say,
He died, was buried, and his tomb
Is with us even today.

2:30 "David was a prophet of God.
He knew God to him had sworn
To seat upon his throne a seed
Who from his line would be born.

2:31 "Foreseeing Christ's resurrection,
What he spoke *we read today,
'He was neither left in Hades,
Nor did His body decay.'

2:32 "This Jesus, God raised up to life.
We have seen this with our eyes.
2:33 Exalted now to God's right hand,
The Spirit He now supplies.

"Having received from the Father
The Holy Spirit as vowed,
That which you now both see and hear,
He has poured among this crowd.

2:34 "For it was not David himself
Who to heaven ascended,
But he himself has said these words
Who of Christ was intended:*

"'Yahweh[164] the Lord said to my Lord,
At My right hand take Your seat
2:35 *Until I make Your enemies*
A footstool for Your own feet.'"

2:36 "Let the house of Israel know
That God has certified
This Jesus as both Lord and Christ,
The One whom you crucified."

2:37 Upon hearing all Peter's words,
Each one's heart was cut right through.
They asked him and the apostles,
"Brothers, what should we all do?"

2:38 Then Peter said to them, "Repent!
Baptism let each receive
Based on the name of Jesus Christ,
Concerning your sins' reprieve.

"The gift of the Holy Spirit
Will come into you to dwell.[165]
2:39 This promise is for all of you
And for your children as well.

"This promise is for all of those
Who live far off from this site,
For anyone that our Lord God
Should to Himself invite."

2:40 Peter warned them with many words
And kept on making this plea:
"Be saved from this generation
That is crooked as can be."

2:41 Then those who had received his word
(About three thousand did obey)
Were baptized in the name of Christ,[166]
Adding to the group that day.

2:42 They continued submitting to
All that the apostles taught.
Also they were giving themselves
To fellowshipping ... a lot.

They'd fellowship by breaking bread
And by praying to the Lord.
2:43 On every single one of them
Amazement was being poured.

Many wonders and many signs
Through the apostles were done.
2:44 All who believed were together
And shared everything as one.

2:45 They were selling their possessions
And even their private land.
They were giving out the proceeds
To every needy hand.

2:46 Every day at the temple courts
They would gather with one mind.
Breaking bread from house to house,
They would share food as they dined.

They did all this with extreme joy,
With sincerity of heart.
While praising God, they found favor
On the community's part.

2:47 Now every day the Lord would add
Those being rescued from sin
To the number already there,
And the number grew therein.*

3:1 Peter and John were going up,
At the ninth hour of the day,
Into the courts of the temple,
The hour many came to pray.

3:2 A certain man, crippled since birth,
Was being carried to the gate,
The entry known as Beautiful
Where he would both beg and wait.

Daily he was brought to the gate
So that he could wait and plead,
Asking people entering the courts
To donate to his need.

3:3 When he saw that Peter and John
Were about to pass him by,
He began begging both of them
To donate from their supply.

3:4 Peter with John then fixed their eyes
On this man who could not walk.
Then Peter said, "Look up at us."
He responded to this talk.

3:5 Expecting to receive from them
Either money or supplies,[x]
The man gave them his attention
By fixing on them his eyes.

3:6 "Silver or gold I don't possess,"
Peter replied to the man,
"But there's one thing I do possess.
So I give you what I can.

"Jesus Christ who's from Nazareth,
I command you in His name
That you get up and walk along.
You now are no longer lame."*

3:7 Then taking him by his right hand,
Peter raised him from his seat.
Immediately he received strength
In his ankles and his feet.

3:8 Jumping about he stood and walked.
Then went with the two inside.
Walking, leaping, and praising God
Was his jubilant stride.

3:9 He was walking and praising God
As all the people took heed.
3:10 They realized that he was the one
Who daily would beg and plead.

He was the one who'd always sit
At the temple's Beautiful Gate.
They were filled with wonder and awe
Because of his current state.

3:11 All the people in great wonder
Together toward them just ran,
At the famed Solomon's Portico,
To see this miracle man.*

The man clung to Peter and John.
The crowd was on every side.
3:12 When Peter saw this assembly,
To the people he replied:

"Why stare at us, men of Israel,
Or why at this do you gawk
As if by our power or virtue
We have caused this man to walk?

3:13 "Abraham, Isaac, and Jacob,
Their God and our fathers' too,
Glorified Jesus, His servant,
The One delivered up by you.

"He is the One that you disowned
To Governor Pilate's face,
Although Pilate had decided
To release Him from your case.

3:14 "This holy, just One you denied,
Asking your wish to be filled
That a killer be given you.
3:15 So the Prince of life you killed.

"But God raised Him up from the dead.
We are witnesses to this word.
3:16 It's upon faith in that One's name
That this man has become cured.

"By Jesus's name he was strengthened,
Whom you see and recognize.
Faith through Jesus restored his health
As you see with your own eyes.

3:17 “Yet now I know that you, brothers,
In ignorance did this thing
Just as also your rulers did
When they crucified the King.*

3:18 “But God fulfilled His word this way,
Which He had before revealed
Through the mouth of all the prophets,
That to suffering His Christ would yield.

3:19 “Therefore, repent and turn to God,
And your sins He will erase.
Do this so that refreshing times
Will come to you from His face.

3:20 “Repent, I say, and turn to God
So that to you He may send
The Christ preselected for you,
That’s Jesus, My King and friend.*

3:21 “It’s necessary for heaven
To receive Jesus the Lord
Until the time that everything
Has become fully restored.

“This season of restoration
God spoke about long ago
Through the mouth of holy prophets,
Recorded for us to know.*

3:22 “For Moses said, ‘From your brothers,
The Lord your God will raise
A prophet who will be like me.
You must heed his every phrase.

3:23 "'For every soul who does not heed
The words that prophet conveys
Will be cut off from the people.'
Moses prophesied these days.[167]

3:24 "All of the prophets from Samuel,
Yes, those that came after him,
Every prophet who spoke announced
These days that we are now in.

3:25 "You are the sons of those prophets
And of the covenant made,
The one your fathers had from God,
Who to Abraham conveyed:

"'Blessings on all earth's families
In your seed will be disbursed.'
3:26 God raised up His servant Jesus
And has sent Him to you first.

"Blessings to you He came to bring
In the turning of each one,
The turning from your wickedness.
That is how the blessings come."*

4:1 During their talk with the people,
Approaching them fast were these:
The captain of the temple guard,
The priests and the Sadducees.

4:2 These were disturbed for the people
By the teaching being said,
By the preaching that in Jesus
There's the rising from the dead.

4:3 They grabbed the men (it was evening),
And they put them under guard.
They held them 'til the morning came,
For their law they had regard.[168]

4:4 Now of the ones who heard the word
To the faith many did come.
Just counting men, the number grew.
About five thousand was that sum.

4:5 The next day in Jerusalem
A large gathering took place.
All their rulers, elders, and scribes
Convened to process the case.*

4:6 Annas the high priest, Caiaphas,
John, Alexander, and more,
All those of high priestly descent
Were gathered on the floor.

4:7 After standing Peter and John
In the center of their ring,
They were asking, "In what power
Or name have you done this thing?"

4:8 Then filled with the Holy Spirit,
Peter before them replied,
"Rulers, elders of the people,
For what are we being tried?*

4:9 "If this day we are being judged
For a good deed that was done
On a weak man that made him whole,
4:10 Let me inform everyone.

"To you and all Israel's people,
Let the truth be known and heard
Just how this man is standing now
Before you completely cured.

"'Twas Jesus Christ of Nazareth,
By His name this man can tread,
Jesus whom you had crucified,
But whom God raised from the dead.

4:11 "He's the stone which was rejected,
Good only to be tossed and thrown,*
Rejected by you the builders,
But became the chief cornerstone.

4:12 "Salvation is in no one else.
No other name will you find,
A name in which we must be saved
That's been given among mankind."

4:13 Seeing Peter and John's boldness,
It defied their explanation,
For they viewed them as untrained men
With no formal education.

They knew full well that with Jesus
These two men had spent their time.
4:14 Seeing the cured man standing there,
They came up with not one crime.

4:15 They ordered them to step outside
For the Sanhedrin to review.
They conferred with one another
4:16 As to just what they should do.

"What should we do about these men?
For all Jerusalem knows
The well-known sign done by these men
Which none of us can oppose.

4:17 "But so that throughout the people
This news will not speed to fame,
Let's threaten them to speak no more
To anyone in this name."

4:18 After the council called them back,
They issued the legal call
That in the name of this Jesus
They not speak or teach at all.

4:19 Peter and John said in response,
"You judge whether it is right
To listen to you over God.
What is lawful in God's sight?

4:20 "For us it is impossible
To keep from spreading the word
About the things which we have seen
And the things which we have heard."

4:21 After more threats, they set them free
Because of the people there.
They found no way to punish them,
And great praises filled the air.*

All the people were praising God
For the sign they did behold.
4:22 The man healed by this miracle,
Was over forty years old.

4:23 Peter and John went to their own
Right after they were released.
They told the group all that was said
By the elders and chief priests.

4:24 After hearing the men's report,
Their voices as one were raised.
Lifting up their voices to God,
These following words they phrased:

"O sovereign Lord, You who have made
The sky, the earth, and the sea,
Also all that is within them,
You ordered this prophecy.*

4:25 "It was through the Holy Spirit
That you spoke this very thing
By the mouth of Your own servant,
Our father, David *the king.

4:26 "'The kings of the earth took their stand.
The rulers gathered as one.
They took their stand against the Lord
And against His Christ, His Son.'[169]

4:27 "For in this city it is true
That they gathered for one point,
Against Your holy servant Jesus
Whom as Christ You did anoint.

"Pontius Pilate and King Herod
Conspired against the Lord.
With Israel's people and Gentiles,
They gathered in one accord.

4:28 "They all gathered to accomplish
Whatever You had preplanned,
All the things that were to happen
By the power of Your hand.

4:29 "So as of now, O Lord, we ask,
Notice the threats they have made.
Grant your bond slaves all the power
To speak Your word unafraid.

4:30 "Do this as Your hand is stretched out
For healings, wonders, and signs.
Through Jesus Your holy servant's name,
Grant our request in these times."*

4:31 After they prayed, where they were at
A great shaking then occurred.
Being filled with the Holy Spirit,
They were boldly speaking God's word.

4:32 Now this great crowd of believers
Was of single heart and mind.
Not one claimed that the things he owned
To his own self was confined.

But everything that each one owned
Were shared in whole or in part.*
They had everything in common,
Being one in mind and heart.

4:33 The apostles with great power
Gave testimony of the Lord,
Namely, Jesus's resurrection.
Upon them great grace was poured.

4:34 For none of them were left in need
Since all owners of homes or lands
Brought the proceeds of what they sold
And released it from their hands.*

4:35 They were placing all the proceeds
Before the apostles' feet.
As anyone was having need,
Their need they would surely meet.

4:36 For instance, Joseph the Levite,
A Cyprian by descent,
Whom the apostles called Barnabas,
Meaning son of encouragement,

4:37 He sold a field which he had owned
And brought all the money back,
Placed it at the apostles' feet
So that there would be no lack.*

5:1 But a man named Ananias,
With his wife Sapphira's consent,
Sold the property that he owned
5:2 But kept back a certain percent.

He brought a part of the proceeds
From the sale of what he owned,
Laid it at the apostles' feet,
And this act his wife condoned.

5:3 But Peter said, "Ananias,
How has Satan filled your heart
To lie to the Holy Spirit,
To keep from the sale a part?

5:4 "Before the sale, who owned the land?
Did it not belong to you?
After the sale you had the right
To decide just what to do.

"So why have you placed in your heart
To carry out this façade?[170]
You did not just lie to people,
But you really lied to God."

5:5 After hearing these very words,
Ananias fell down dead.
Everyone who heard about this,
Great fear upon them was spread.

5:6 The younger men, then getting up,
Wrapped Ananias with care.
After bringing his body out,
They then buried him somewhere.

5:7 About three hours of time had passed
When his wife had entered in.
Now she was not aware at all
Just what had happened to him.

5:8 Peter answered by asking her,
"Tell me, is this the right count
From the sale of your property?"
She said, "Yes, that's the amount."

5:9 Peter came before her and said,
"It was agreed by you two
To test the Spirit of the Lord.
Why this thing did you both do?

"Behold, the feet of those young men,
Who buried that man of yours,
Are approaching the entrance way
To bring you also outdoors."

5:10 At once she fell dead at his feet.
The younger men to her ran.
They found her dead, carried her out,
And buried her by her man.

5:11 Great fear fell on the entire church
And on everyone who heard
About these things that just took place,
About all that had occurred.

5:12 By means of the apostles' hands
Among the people were done
Many wonders and many signs,
And they met together as one.

Now in Solomon's Portico
Was where they would normally be,
5:13 But the others dared not join them
Though praised by the community.

5:14 Yet crowds believing in the Lord
(Not just men but women too)
Kept on increasing all the more.
The numbers just grew and grew.*

5:15 This caused people to carry out
Into the wide streets the ill
And place them on cots and pallets
So as their hopes to fulfill.*

They hoped that at the very least
Whenever Peter walked past,
That upon any one of them
His shadow might be cast.

5:16 From Jerusalem's nearby towns,
The crowd gathered at will,
Bringing those vexed by unclean spirits,
And bringing also their ill.

Now all of these were being healed,
5:17 But envy came to infect
The high priest and all those with him,
Sadducees, *a Jewish sect.

5:18 They rose against the apostles
For the purpose to prevail.
They laid their hands upon them all
And put them in public jail.

5:19 But an angel of the Lord came
During the night to their aid
And pushed open the prison door.
He led them out and conveyed:

5:20 "Keep on going and keep speaking.
In the temple stand your ground.
Tell the people the whole message
Of this life *and where it's found."

5:21 After hearing the angel's words,
Just as soon as it was dawn,
They came into the temple courts
And were teaching on and on.

Now the high priest and those with him,
The Sanhedrin they did call
With the council of Israel's sons,
Not just some of them but all.

As soon as all were gathered there,
Certain officers were told
To bring from jail the apostles,
And so to the jail they strolled.

5:22 When they arrived at the prison,
The apostles weren't around.
So they returned to the council
And reported what they found.

5:23 "We found the jail securely locked,
At the doors, the guards in place.
Unlocking it, we looked inside
And saw no one, not a trace."

5:24 The captain of the temple guard
And the chief priests were perplexed
Upon hearing all of these words
As to what would happen next.

5:25 Then someone came and said to them,
"The men you had jailed, behold!
They are standing in the temple
Teaching the people, *how bold!"

5:26 The captain with his officers
Departed to bring them back.
Fearing the people might stone them,
Coercion they did lack.

5:27 After bringing the men back in,
They had the apostles stand
In the midst of the Sanhedrin,
For answers they did demand.

The high priest asked for a response,
5:28 "We charged you all to abstain
From teaching any words at all
By using that one Man's name.

"But you have filled Jerusalem
With your teaching, as you see.
Do you plan to make this Man's blood
Our responsibility?"

5:29 Peter replying to their charge
With all the apostles said,
"It's essential to obey God
And not obey men instead.

5:30 “Jesus whom you killed with your hands
By hanging Him on a tree,
The God of our own forefathers
Raised Him up from death’s decree.

5:31 “God exalted to His right hand
This One as Chief and Savior
To grant repentance to Israel
And pardon for misbehavior.

5:32 “We’re witnesses of all these things.
The Holy Spirit is too,
Whom God has given to the ones
Who to Him are faithful and true.”

5:33 As they listened, they filled with rage,
And them they counseled to kill,
5:34 But one in the Sanhedrin stood,
A man named Gamaliel.

Gamaliel was a Pharisee
And a teacher of the Law.
All the people respected him,
And he had the men withdraw.

He ordered them to be put outside
Just for a little while.
5:35 The Sanhedrin he then addressed
Concerning these men on trial.*

“Israelite men, inspect yourselves
About those men *and their ways.
As to what you intend to do,
Remember the former days.

5:36 "Theudas arose some time ago,
Claiming to be someone then.
To this one a number were joined,
A crowd of four hundred men.

"Theudas was killed, was put to death,
And everyone was scattered,
As many as were swayed by him.
So from this nothing mattered.

5:37 "After this another man came.
It was Judas from Galilee.
'Twas in the days of the census
That he caused an apostasy.

"People departed after him,
But Judas was killed also.
As many as by him were swayed,
All were dispersed to and fro.

5:38 "I now tell you, stand back from them
And just leave these men alone.
If from men comes this plan or work,
It will then be overthrown.

5:39 "But if from God this all derives,
Them you will not overthrow,
But you'd be found opposing God.
So let's just let these men go."*

5:40 Therefore, they were convinced by him
And called the apostles in.
They punished them by beating them.
Then ordered them once again.

They said that the name of Jesus
Could not be used any day
Whenever they speak, preach, or teach,
And then they sent them away.

5:41 Rejoicing, they were going out
From the Sanhedrin's face
Since for His name they were esteemed
Worthy to suffer disgrace.

5:42 But daily in the temple courts,
And from house to house as well,
The good news that Jesus is Christ
They were not ceasing to tell.

6:1 When the numbers of disciples
Were increasing in those days,
A complaint arose by the Jews
Who were of the Grecian ways.

Against the Hebrew-speaking Jews
This complaint was directed,
For when the food was served each day,
Greek widows were neglected.

6:2 The Twelve summoned altogether
The crowd of disciples and said,
"It's wrong for us to neglect God's word
In order to distribute bread.

6:3 "Brothers, select from among you
Good men in word and in deed,
Seven wise and Spirit-filled men
Who we can charge with this need.

6:4 "But we ourselves must continue
To devote ourselves with care
To the service of God's message
And to the matters of prayer."

6:5 This solution pleased the whole group.
So seven* they selected:
Stephen, a man of faithfulness
Whom the Spirit directed,[171]

Philip, Prochorus, Nicanor,
Timon, and Parmenas too,
Then Nicholas from Antioch,
A Greek that became a Jew.

6:6 These seven men were brought to stand
Before the apostles who prayed.
As they offered this prayer to God,
Upon them their hands they laid.

6:7 The word of God kept on spreading.
The disciples' number grew.
The number in Jerusalem
Just multiplied through and through.

Now there came to obedience
To the faith *that these were taught,
Some of the priests in that city,
And that number was a lot.

6:8 Among the people Stephen came
Full of power and of grace.
He was working many wonders
And great signs in every place.

6:9 But certain ones called Libertines,
Who had their own synagogue,
Came and stood opposed to Stephen,
Engaging in dialogue.

Cyrene and Alexandrian,
Cilician and Asian,
Comprised this group in dialogue
On this historic occasion.*

6:10 Yet together they lacked the strength
To stand against his teaching,
Against wisdom and the Spirit
By which Stephen was preaching.

6:11 So then they had men testify
After a secretive prod,
"We have heard him speak blasphemies
Against Moses, also God."

6:12 The people, elders, and the scribes
Were then moved to take this course:
To bring him to the Sanhedrin.
So they dragged him there by force.

6:13 False witnesses arose to say,
"This man continues to jaw,
Speaking against this holy place
And speaking against the Law.

6:14 "For we've heard him say that Jesus
(That Nazarene of disgrace)[172]
Will change the Mosaic customs
And destroy this very place."

6:15 Those sitting on the Sanhedrin
Stared at Stephen *to condemn,
But like the face of an angel,
Stephen's face appeared to them.

7:1 The high priest asked, "Are these things so?"
7:2 He answered them to convince:
"Brothers, fathers, listen to me.
O men, please hear my defense.

"The God of glory showed Himself
To our father Abraham
While in Mesopotamia
Before living in Haran.

7:3 "He said to him, 'Leave your country.
Leave your relatives and go.
Travel to another country,
A land which to you I'll show.'

7:4 "From the Chaldean land he came,
But Haran he settled in.
From there, after his father died,
God removed him once again.

"He brought him to this very land,
The land in which you're now found,
7:5 But gave him no inheritance,
Not even a foot of ground.

"And even when he had no child,
To him God promised to give
And to his offspring after him
This land in which you now live.

7:6 "God spoke in this way: 'In a land
That would not be theirs to own,
His offspring would be aliens,
And in slavery they would groan.

"'For they would work under hardship,*
But never as volunteers.*
Enslaved they would be mistreated
For about four hundred years.

7:7 "'To the nation that would enslave,'
God said, 'I will judge that race.
After that I will bring them out,
And they'll serve Me in this place.'

7:8 "And then God gave to Abraham
This covenantal provision:
That every male descendant born*
Must receive circumcision.

"Thus, Abraham fathered Isaac
And did just as he was told.
His son Isaac he circumcised
When he was just eight days old.

“Later Isaac fathered Jacob,
And Jacob, the twelve patriarchs
7:9 Who sold Joseph into Egypt,
Moved by their jealous remarks.

7:10 “But God saved him from all hardships.
With God’s presence he was equipped.
He gave him grace, also wisdom,
Before Pharaoh, King of Egypt.

“Pharaoh made him to rule Egypt,
Not just in part but the whole.*
Over his entire palace
He gave him complete control.

7:11 “Then there came on all of Egypt,
And Canaan, this did include,
A famine that was so severe,
Our fathers weren’t finding food.

7:12 “When Jacob heard that there was grain
In the Egyptian nation,
Our ancestors he sent ahead
On their first visitation.

7:13 “The second time that they were sent,
Joseph’s face was then revealed
To his brothers from whom before
His own face he had concealed.[173]

“After Pharaoh learned of these kin,
7:14 Joseph sent them back to call
His father Jacob, every kin,
Seventy-five souls in all.

7:15 "Jacob went down from where he lived
To Egypt so as to dwell.
He himself died in Egypt's land.
Our fathers died there as well.

7:16 "Then to Shechem they were removed,
Placed in a burial plot
Which from Hamor's sons in Shechem
Abraham with silver had bought.

7:17 "When the promised time was nearing
That to Abraham God made known,[174]
Our people were greatly increased.
In Egypt their number had grown.

7:18 "They grew until another king,
Who of Joseph did not know,
Arose to rule over Egypt
7:19 And ordered them not to grow.*

"He persecuted our fathers.
Against them he did connive
By making them leave their babies
So that they would not survive.

7:20 "In that season Moses was born.
Now to God he was sublime.
He was raised in his father's house
For a three-month span of time.

7:21 "After he had been placed outside,
Pharaoh's daughter saw this one.
She picked him up for her own self
And raised him to be her son.

7:22 "Moses was trained in Egypt's ways,
In wisdom of every kind.
Mighty in words and in his works
Was how Moses was defined.

7:23 "When he became forty years old,
It impressed upon his heart
To view his brothers, Israel's sons,
From whom he had been apart.*

7:24 "He saw one being mistreated
And went to stand in his stead.
He avenged him who was oppressed,
Striking the Egyptian dead.

7:25 "He was thinking that his brothers
Would believe that by his hand
God was giving to them release,
But they did not understand.

7:26 "On the next day he intervened
Between two men in a brawl.
He tried to bring them into peace,
But they listened not at all.*

"He said, 'O men! Brothers you are,
Why do you harm each other?'
7:27 But one of them pushed him aside
(The one harming his brother).

"He said, 'O you! Are you ruler?
Who assigned you to this task?
Who assigned you to be our judge?
I have one more thing to ask.*

7:28 "'Do you wish to murder me too
And do this in the same way
As you murdered the Egyptian
Which took place just yesterday?'

7:29 "At that remark, Moses ran off.
As a stranger he did fare.
He lived in the land of Midian
And fathered two sons while there.

7:30 "When forty years had finally passed,
Into view an angel came
In the desert of Mt. Sinai,
In a fiery bush's flame.

7:31 "When Moses saw this puzzling[175] sight,
He was totally amazed.
As he went to look more closely,
The Lord's voice came from what blazed.

7:32 "'I am the God of your fathers.
I'm the God of Abraham,
The God of Isaac and Jacob.
Yes, their God I Myself am.'

"Moses trembled and dared not look.
His approach he did not complete.[176]
7:33 Then the Lord God instructed him,
'Take the sandals off your feet.

"'For holy ground is before you,
The same place on which you stand.
7:34 I've surely seen the oppression
Of My people in Egypt's land.

"'I have come down to rescue them.
I have heard all of their sighs.
Let Me send you into Egypt.
I command you, now arise.'

7:35 "This Moses whom they rejected
By questioning his intent
To be their ruler and their judge,
He is the one whom God sent.

"As their ruler and redeemer,
To Egypt Moses then came
With the hand of the angel
Who appeared in the bush's *flame.

7:36 "He led them out by doing signs
And wonders in Egypt's land,
In the Red Sea, then the desert.
About forty years this spanned.

7:37 "This is the Moses who addressed
The Israelites in those days,
'From your brothers and for your sakes,
A prophet like me God will raise.'

7:38 "He was in the assembly with
Our fathers in the desert dry
And with the angel who spoke to him
On the mountain called Sinai.

"He received the living sayings
To pass on to us to hear,
7:39 But our fathers did not desire
To give him a listening ear.

“Instead they pushed Moses aside,
And in their hearts they returned
Into Egypt from which they came.
7:40 For other gods they then yearned.*

“They told Aaron, ‘Make for us gods
That can lead us *at our whim.
Moses who led us from Egypt,
We know not what’s happened to him.’

7:41 “So in those days they made a calf.
Offerings to the calf they brought,
And in the works of their own hands
They were rejoicing a lot.

7:42 “God turned away and gave them up
To worship the stars of the sky.
As in the scroll of the prophets
Is written this charge from on high:

“‘The sacrifices and offerings
Which, O Israel, you had brought
While in the desert forty years,
Were they for Me? They were not!

7:43 “‘Because you carried Molech’s tent
And Rephan’s star as your god,
Idols that you made for worship,
I will remove you abroad.

“‘Past the borders of Babylon,
I will carry you away
Because you worshipped other gods*
Instead of Me in that day.’*

7:44 “They had God’s tent in the desert
(The Witness as it was known),
Which God ordered Moses to make
Like the model he was shown.

7:45 “In turn our fathers after them,
With Joshua this tent they brought
Into the land of the Gentiles
Which to them God would allot.*

“Before the face of our fathers,
God just drove them out somewhere.
So in the land ’til David’s days
The Tent of Witness was there.

7:46 “David asked God if he could build,
(for in God’s eyes he found grace),
If he could build for Jacob’s house
A permanent dwelling place.

7:47 “Solomon built a house for God,
7:48 But the Most High does not dwell
In places made by human hands
As this prophet goes on to tell:

7:49 “‘This is what the Lord God declares:
The universe is My throne.
The earth, a footstool for My feet.
How can you build Me a home?

“‘*What kind of home will you build Me?*
Where will My resting place be?
7:50 *Has not My hand made all these things,*
This heaven and earth you see?’”*

7:51 "Stiff-necked people! Uncircumcised!
That is, in your hearts and ears,
You always oppose God's[177] Spirit
Like your fathers did those years.

7:52 "Of the prophets, tell me which one,
Your fathers did not pursue?
They even killed those who foretold,
'The Just One's coming to you.'

"Traitors, killers you've now become,
For Him you killed and betrayed.
7:53 The Law as ordained by angels
You received but disobeyed!"

7:54 As they were hearing all these things,
In their hearts they were enraged
Against Stephen, and with their teeth
In gnashing they then engaged.

7:55 But full of the Holy Spirit,
Staring into heaven's height,
He saw God's glory, then Jesus
Standing by God on His right.

7:56 "Behold," he said, "I'm observing,
Heaven being opened wide!
I'm observing the Son of Man
Whose standing at God's right side!"

7:57 But crying out with a loud voice,
They covered their ears and ran.
As one mob, they rushed upon him,
Having an impulsive plan.*

7:58 Dragging him out of the city,
They were stoning him in gall.
The witnesses threw down their robes
At a young man's feet named Saul.

7:59 "O Lord Jesus, take my spirit!"
This, while being stoned, he cried;
7:60 Then kneeling he said, "Lord, don't charge
These men with this sin." Then died.

8:1 Saul was consenting to his death.
So in that day there was cast
Against the church in Jerusalem
Persecution that was vast.

In the region of Judea
And also Samaria,
They were strewn, save the apostles,
Who remained in the area.

8:2 Prior to this, a group of men
That were considered devout
Buried Stephen, and upon him
Intense weeping they poured out.

8:3 By barging into all their homes,
The church Saul began to assail.
Dragging the men and the women,
He was throwing them into jail.

8:4 Therefore, the church that was scattered
Was going from place to place
Proclaiming to all the good news,
The message about God's grace.*

8:5 Going down to Samaria,
The city *that is to say,
Philip was announcing to them
Concerning the Christ one day.

8:6 In harmony the multitudes,
As the signs they saw and heard
That Philip was performing there,
Were glued to his every word.

8:7 For many were demon-possessed,
And spirits were being expelled,
But this was not done quietly,
For while coming out, they yelled.

Many were lame and paralyzed,
But they were completely cured.
8:8 In that city joy overflowed
For all that they saw and heard.*

8:9 A certain man known as Simon
Had done magic as of late,
Amazing the Samaritans,
Claiming to be someone great.

8:10 Now all of them, the great and small,
Were glued to what he had done,
Saying, "This is the power of God,
The power called the Mighty One."

8:11 They were so drawn to him because
For such a long duration
He had amazed them with his feats
Of magic in that location.

8:12 But upon believing Philip
(Men and women this comprised)
For proclaiming the gospel news,
They all were being baptized.

Philip preached about God's kingdom
And about Jesus Christ's name.
8:13 Even Simon believed his words.
To be baptized Simon came.

After Simon had been baptized,
He followed Philip around.
Great powers and signs he saw done.
By amazement he was bound.

8:14 The apostles in Jerusalem
Heard that God's word was upon
Samaritans who had received.
So they sent Peter and John.

8:15 When they came down, they prayed for them,
For the Spirit had yet to fall
On any of them who believed.[178]
So they petitioned for them all.

They prayed that the Holy Spirit
On each of them would be poured,
8:16 For they had only been baptized,
In the name of Jesus, the Lord.

8:17 Now as they laid their hands on them,
The Spirit they each received.
Simon saw the Spirit bestowed
Upon all those who believed.

8:18 He saw that this was by the touch
Of the apostolic hand
That the Spirit had been given.
So this power he did demand.

Offering money he said to them,
8:19 "Give me this power to clutch,
So that I may give the Spirit
To anyone whom I touch."

8:20 But Peter answered back to him,
"May your silver with you die
Since you thought God's gift could be bought
By the money you supply.

8:21 "You have no portion in this thing,
Not even the smallest part,
For in the presence of our God
You are not upright in heart.

8:22 "Therefore, repent from this your wrong,
And to the Lord start praying.
Perhaps He will forgive you for
What your heart is conveying.

8:23 "I observe that you're filled with gall.
Bitterness in your heart reigns,
And I perceive that you are in
Unrighteous and wicked chains."

8:24 But Simon said, replying back,
"You pray for me to the Lord
So nothing will come upon me,
None of what you've underscored."

8:25 They returned to Jerusalem,
Peter and John, *that is to say,
After they spoke and testified
Of the Lord's message that day.

They were preaching the gospel news
As they journeyed to their town,
Stopping in many villages
Where Samaritans were found.

8:26 The Lord's angel told Philip, "Rise!
Go south to the road that leads
From Jerusalem to Gaza"
(Which through a desert proceeds).

8:27 So rising up he journeyed south,
And into his view, behold!
An Ethiopian eunuch
Traveling on the same road.

By the Ethiopian queen,
The Candace, as she was known,
He was given authority
Over all that was her own.

He had gone to Jerusalem
In order to worship there,
8:28 And now he was returning home,
Reading the Scriptures with care.*

While seated in his chariot,
He was reading from the Word,
From the prophet named Isaiah,
8:29 When Philip the Spirit stirred.

"Go now and join this chariot,"
To Philip the Spirit said.
8:30 As Philip neared the chariot,
He heard what was being read.

As he heard the eunuch reading
What in Isaiah was penned,
He asked, "Those words you are reading,
Do you really comprehend?"

8:31 "How can I understand at all,"
To him the eunuch replied,
"Unless there were to be someone
That to me would be a guide?"

He called Philip to sit with him.
The chariot Philip boarded.
8:32 Here's the passage he was reading,
A Scripture long recorded:*

"He's like a sheep led to slaughter
And like a lamb being shaved
Who's silent before its shearer.
So noise from His mouth He waived.

8:33 "His judgment was taken away
In His humiliation.
Since His life was snatched from the earth,
Who'll speak of His generation?"

8:34 Now the eunuch questioned Philip,
"The prophet, he speaks of whom,
About himself or someone else?
What person should I presume?"

8:35 Philip opened his mouth and spoke,
Starting from the Scripture read,
And told him the news of Jesus,
Of Him rising from the dead.*

8:36 Traveling along they neared water,
And so the eunuch surmised,
"Look! There's water. What's stopping me?
Why shouldn't I be baptized?"[179]

8:38 He told the chariot to stop.
Into the water they began
(Philip as well as the eunuch).
Then Philip baptized this man.

8:39 When they came up from the water,
The Lord's Spirit snatched away
Philip from the eunuch's presence
Who saw him no more that day.

The eunuch went his way with joy,
8:40 But Philip was found elsewhere.
Philip was found in Azotus,
Many miles away from there.[180]

Philip traveled to all the towns
As he made the gospel known
Until he reached Caesarea,
The place where he made his home.[181]

9:1 Still breathing both threats and murder,
On disciples of the Lord,
To the high priest Saul went and asked
That some letters they record.

9:2 To the Damascus synagogues
Letters were to be addressed.
All those belonging to the Way
Saul could legally arrest.

Both men and women of the Way
Saul had all power to bind
And bring them to Jerusalem,
Every person he could find.

9:3 Now on his way to Damascus
As he was nearing the town,
Without warning from heaven came
A light that flashed all around.

9:4 As he fell down upon the ground,
He heard a voice to him speak,
"O Saul, O Saul, why against Me
Persecution do you seek?"

9:5 Saul replied back, "Sir, please answer,
What is your identity?"
"I am Jesus," was the reply,
"You are persecuting Me!

9:6 "But get up and enter the town,
And you yourself will receive
Guidance as to what you must do.
Now get up from here and leave."*

9:7 Now the men had stood there speechless
(The ones traveling with Saul).
Although able to hear the noise,
They saw no one there at all.

9:8 Saul then rose up from off the ground.
To Christ's command he resigned.*
Although his eyes had been opened,
He saw nothing. He was blind.

Into Damascus by the hand,
Those with him guided his feet.
9:9 For three days he was without sight.
Neither did he drink or eat.

9:10 A disciple in Damascus,
To him in a vision came
The Lord who was calling to him.
Ananias was his name.

The Lord called out, "Ananias!"
"I am here, Lord," he said,
9:11 "Get up!" the Lord commanded him,
"To this place you now must head.

"Go to the street that is called Straight.
Search for a man who's praying.
His name will be Saul of Tarsus.
In Judas's house he's staying.

9:12 "He already knows you by name.
In a vision he saw it all.
You came in and laid hands on him
To restore the sight of Saul."

9:13 Ananias said in reply,
"From many, Lord, I have heard
How much evil this man has done.
Persecution he has stirred.*

"All the saints in Jerusalem,
All those whom are set apart,
This man Saul has persecuted.
He's had murder on his heart.*

9:14 "From the chief priests he has secured
The authority to bind
Everyone who worships Your name,
All he is able to find."[182]

9:15 The Lord replied, "Get going now.
My chosen vessel is Saul
To take My name to Gentiles, kings,
And Israel's sons, to all.

9:16 "For I Myself will show to him,
Yes, to him I will make plain
The many things he must suffer
On behalf of My own name."

9:17 Ananias then left from there
And entered into the home.
As he laid his hands upon him,
To him these words he made known:

"The Lord sent me, O brother Saul,
The same Jesus seen by you
During your travel on the road,
For a purpose, *namely two.

"He has sent me so that your sight
Will be completely restored
And so that you'll be filled by Him,
The Holy Spirit of the Lord."

9:18 Something like scales fell from Saul's eyes.
Right then his sight was renewed.
9:19 He got up and then was baptized
And gained strength by eating food.

Sometime later in Damascus
(Three years, as Galatians conveys),[183]
Saul stayed with the disciples there,
And he stayed for several days.

9:20 Right away in the synagogues
He was proclaiming the news
That Jesus is the Son of God,
9:21 Which was amazing the Jews.

All those listening were questioning,
"Isn't he one and the same
With him who in Jerusalem
Attacked callers on that name?

"Isn't this man one and the same
With him who had come to town
So as to bring to the chief priests
Those worshippers fully bound?"

9:22 However, Saul was growing strong
And was confounding the Jews
Who were living in Damascus
By arguing the good news.

He was proving Him as the Christ,
9:23 But when many days had spanned,
The Jews plotted to destroy him,
9:24 But Saul learned what they had planned.

Now day and night they were watching.
On the gates they kept their eye,
Waiting for him to leave their town
So his death they could supply.

9:25 But then one night his disciples
Took him through the city wall
By carefully letting him down
In a basket that was not small.

9:26 When he entered Jerusalem,
He tried to associate
With the disciples that were there,
But their fear of him was great.

All of them were afraid of him
And not one of them believed
That he was a true disciple.
Therefore, Saul was not received.*

9:27 To the apostles Saul was brought
By Barnabas who then told
How Saul had seen the risen Lord
While traveling on the road.

He told them that the Lord had talked
To Saul in words that were plain.
He told them that in Damascus
Saul spoke boldly in Jesus's name.

9:28 So Saul began staying with them
And was going in and out
Of the city Jerusalem,
Spreading the Lord's name about.

9:29 He was speaking to Hellenists,
Engaging in great debate,
But they were seeking all the more
His death to negotiate.

9:30 When the brothers learned about this,
To Saul they directly went.
They took him down to Caesarea.
Then to Tarsus him they sent.

9:31 Therefore, the church was having peace
Throughout the whole area,
In the regions of Judea,
Galilee, and Samaria.

Since the church was being edified
And lived in the fear of the Lord
And in the Holy Spirit's help,
The number of disciples soared.

9:32 Sometime later, as Peter went
Through all the land everywhere,
He came to the town of Lydda
To see the saints living there.

9:33 He found a man named Aeneas,
Who in his bed had remained
For the span of about eight years.
Paralysis had him chained.

9:34 To him Peter said, "Aeneas!
Jesus Christ heals you today.
Get up and make your bed right now!"
And he stood up right away.

9:35 Everyone who witnessed this man
As one completely restored,
Who lived in Lydda and Sharon,
Were converted to the Lord.

9:36 A disciple named Tabitha,
Which is Dorcas in the Greek,
Was full of good works in Joppa
And practiced helping the weak.

9:37 It came about in those same days
That she fell sick and then died.
They washed her up and then placed her
In a room high up inside.

9:38 Now Joppa was close to Lydda,
And the disciples had heard
That Peter was in Joppa then.
So with two men they sent word.

They requested that Peter come,
And to come without delay.
9:39 As soon as Peter heard their words,
He went with them right away.

Arriving there, they took Peter
To the room high up inside.
All the widows stood around him,
Showing him things as they cried.

They showed him things that Dorcas made
The time she had been around,
The inner clothes and outer clothes.
With much grief they did abound.*

9:40 Peter forced them outside the room.
Kneeling, he prayed to the Lord.
He turned toward the body and said,
"Tabitha, rise! You're restored!"

She opened up her eyes right then,
And seeing him, up she sat.
9:41 Peter gave her a helping hand
And raised her up just like that.

Calling for the saints and widows,
He showed her alive, restored.
9:42 This news spread through all of Joppa,
And many trusted the Lord.

9:43 So in Joppa for many days
The apostle Peter stayed
As a guest of one named Simon
Who was a tanner by trade.

10:1 In Caesarea was a man,
Cornelius, who had command
As a Roman centurion
Over an Italian band.

10:2 He was godly, and he feared God.
Yes, Israel's God he extolled.*
This was not only true of him
But of his entire household.

He would practice giving money
Generously to those in need.
He would practice giving prayers.
Continually to God he'd plead.

10:3 In a vision he clearly saw,
In the ninth hour of the day,
God's angel coming up to him.
"Cornelius!" he heard him say.

10:4 Cornelius stared right at him,
But greatly engulfed by fear,
He said, "Yes, sir, what do you want?"
As the angel was coming near.

Answering him, the angel said,
"Your prayers and gifts to the poor
Have been as a memorial
Since God they have come before.

10:5 "Send out some men into Joppa.
Do it now. Do not postpone.
Have them fetch a man named Simon,
But as Peter he is known.

10:6 "Peter is a guest of Simon,
The well-known tanner, his host.
The house is easy to detect.
It's located on the coast."

10:7 Once the angel who spoke to him
Had departed from his face,
Cornelius then right away
Summoned three men for this case.

Two were household servants of his,
One, a soldier of his band
Who always accompanied him
And was godly in his stand.

10:8 After he had explained to them
Everything he saw and heard,
He sent these three onto Joppa
To fulfill the angel's word.*

10:9 The next day while on their journey,
In the sixth hour of the day,
As they drew close to the city,
Peter went on the roof to pray.

10:10 Sometime later he hungered much
And desired to eat some food.
While they prepared the meal for him,
A trance overtook his mood.

10:11 He saw the sky as opened up,
Then an object coming down.
It was like one gigantic sheet
Being lowered to the ground.

By its corners, which numbered four,
It was lowered to the ground.
10:12 It was holding some animals.
With many it did abound.

Four-footed beasts of every kind,
As well as birds of the air,
Every kind of earthly reptile
Were in that huge sheet somewhere.

10:13 Then there occurred a distinct noise,
But it wasn't from the sheet.*
"Peter," a voice commanded him,
"Now get up and kill and eat!"

10:14 But Peter said, "I cannot, Lord,
For some are profane, unclean.
I have never eaten such things,
The forbidden things, I mean.[184]

10:15 Again there came a voice to him,
The voice which he heard before,
"Whatever God has purified,
Don't call profane anymore."

10:16 Now this happened exactly thrice.
Then the object with its supply,
Immediately, right afterward,
Was snatched up into the sky.

10:17 As Peter was thinking about
The vision's correlation,
The men sent by Cornelius
Had learned of his location.

Upon coming to Simon's house,
They stopped at the entrance door
10:18 And asked whether Simon Peter
Was a guest there anymore.

10:19 Now the Spirit said to Peter,
While he was still deep in thought,
"Behold, three men are seeking you.
10:20 Get up and hesitate not.

"Proceed downstairs, and go with them
Without one bias or bent
Because these are the messengers,
The three I Myself have sent."

10:21 He went downstairs, telling the men,
"I am the one whom you seek.
For what reason have you all come?"
10:22 And the men began to speak.

"Cornelius, a centurion,
A righteous, God-fearing man,
Respected by the Jewish world
Is obeying God's command.

"A holy angel ordered him
To summon you to his home
And to listen to all your words.
So to you we make this known."*

10:23 Calling them in, Peter lodged them
Since it was late in the day.
The next morning when he got up,
With the men he went away.

Going with Peter on this trip,
From Joppa were some brothers.
10:24 They arrived at Caesarea
The next day with the others.

Cornelius, having gathered
His kinfolk and friends who were dear,
Was already waiting for them.
10:25 He bowed down as Peter drew near.

Prostrated before Peter's feet,
To worship him he began,
10:26 But raising him up, Peter said,
"Stand up! I am just a man."

10:27 As he was conversing with him,
Peter went with him inside
And saw the many gathered there.
10:28 With these words he then replied:

"You know our custom very well
For a man who is a Jew.
To join or visit foreigners
Is considered a taboo.

"But God has made it clear to me
That no man is to be named
One who is profane or unclean
Because of the race he's claimed.

10:29 "Because of this, I came along
Without one hesitation.
For what reason have you called me?
What is your explanation?"

10:30 Cornelius replied to him,
"Four days ago from this time,
I was praying in my own home.
The hour of the day was nine.

"Behold, this man stood before me
In clothing that was splendid.
10:31 He said to me, 'Cornelius,
Your prayer has ascended.

"'It has been heard by God Himself,
And your gifts to those in need
Have been remembered in God's sight.
Therefore, this you now must heed.*

10:32 "'Send out some men into Joppa.
Do it now. Do not postpone.
Have them fetch a man named Simon,
But as Peter he is known.

"'Peter is a guest of Simon,
The well-known tanner, his host.
The house is easy to detect.
It's located on the coast.'

10:33 "Immediately, I sent for you,
And in coming you have done well.
Now we stand before God to hear
All the Lord has told you to tell."

10:34 Peter opened his mouth and said,
"To this truth I now relate:
That between races and nations
God does not discriminate.

10:35 "But in every race and nation
The one who fears God above
And works the deeds of righteousness
Is welcome by God *who's love.

10:36 "The word He sent to Israel's sons.
The good news of peace was preached
Through Jesus Christ who's Lord of all.
10:37 Your ears this gospel has reached.

"You know that throughout Judea,
Beginning from Galilee,
After the baptism John preached,
This message spread rapidly.

10:38 "How this Jesus from Nazareth,
With the Holy Spirit and might,
Was anointed by God Himself,
And God was with Him, all right.

"He went about doing good deeds,
And everyone whom He found
That was oppressed by the Devil
He healed, making them sound.

10:39 "We're witnesses of all He did,
Both in the land of the Jews
And the city Jerusalem,
*Where His own life He would lose.

"There they sentenced Jesus to death
By hanging Him on a tree,
10:40 But God raised Him on the third day,
Presenting Him openly.

10:41 "He was not shown to everyone,
Just to witnesses whom God chose,
To us who ate and drank with Him
After from the dead He rose.

10:42 "He ordered us to announce this
And to testify abroad
That over the living and the dead
He's the judge ordained by God.

10:43 "All the prophets attest of Him,
That whoever in Him believes,
Through His name concerning all sins,
Forgiveness that person receives."

10:44 Peter was still speaking these words
When the Holy Spirit fell
Upon all those hearing the word,
10:45 And amazement did excel.

For the circumcised believers
That came with Peter could see
The Holy Spirit on Gentiles
Being given generously.

10:46 They also heard the Gentiles speak
In tongues, exalting God on high.
So Peter said, "To be baptized
In water who can deny?

"They've received the Holy Spirit
Just as we received before.
10:47 We can't refuse to baptize them
Into water anymore."

10:48 He ordered them to be baptized
In the Lord Jesus Christ's name.
With begging they convinced Peter
For a few days to remain.

11:1 The brothers throughout Judea
And the other apostles heard
That the Gentiles also received
The good message of God's word.

11:2 When coming to Jerusalem,
Peter was challenged to his face
By those of the circumcision
Who were of the Jewish race.*

11:3 “You went to uncircumcised men,
And you entered into their home
And even ate a meal with them,”
They said *with an accusing tone.

11:4 Peter began giving to them
An account of what occurred
In the order that it happened.
The following was his word:

11:5 “I was in the town of Joppa
When into a trance I fell.
While I was engaged in prayer,
This vision I saw and now tell:

“A certain object from the sky
That looked like a great big sheet
Was lowered by its four corners,
Coming right down to my feet.

11:6 “Into this sheet I was looking,
Staring at all that was there.
I saw all the earth’s animals
And all the birds of the air.

“All the four-footed animals
Were right there in that great sheet,
All the reptiles and the wild beasts.
11:7 Then a voice told me to eat.

“‘Arise, Peter! Slaughter and eat!’
11:8 I said, ‘Lord, I must refrain.
I’ve never eaten anything
That is unclean or profane.’

11:9 "A second time a voice then spoke
From heaven with this reply,
'Don't ever consider profane
That which God does purify.'

11:10 "Now this happened exactly thrice,
Then the object with its supply,
Immediately, right afterward,[185]
Was drawn up into the sky.

11:11 "Right then and there three men arrived
At the place in which we stayed,
Sent to me from Caesarea
Sometime before I had prayed.[186]

11:12 "The Spirit said to go with them.
No bias was I to own.
Those six brothers went there with me,
And we entered the man's home.

11:13 "He informed us how he had seen
An angel inside his place,
Commanding him what he must do
While standing before his face.

"'Send out some men into Joppa.
Do it now. Do not postpone.[187]
Have them fetch a man named Simon,
But as Peter he is known.

11:14 "'Peter will speak some words to you.
You'll be saved by what you hear,
Not just you, but all your household
As the words enter the ear.'*

11:15 "When I began to speak to them,
The Holy Spirit on them fell
In the same way He came on us
At Pentecost to indwell.[188]

11:16 "I recalled the Lord's word to us,
'In water John baptized you,
But soon in the Holy Spirit
You all will be baptized too.'

11:17 "So, since this gift God gave to them
Who trusted Jesus the Lord,[189]
Who am I that I can stop God
Who the same gift on us poured?"

11:18 Hearing these words, they fell silent.
Then they praised God without strife,
"God has granted to the Gentiles
Repentance that leads to life!"

11:19 Now those who were scattered about
Due to the tribulation,
Which arose because of Stephen,
Had progressed in their migration.

They reached as far as Phoenicia
And Cyprus and Antioch,
Speaking the word to all the Jews,
But to Gentiles they would not talk.

11:20 But some men came to Antioch
From Cyprus and from Cyrene,
Preaching about the Lord Jesus
To the Greeks whom they had seen.

11:21 The Lord's hand was with those who preached
So that Greeks in numbers vast
Turned to the Lord as believers,
And news of this traveled fast.[190]

11:22 Now the church in Jerusalem
Had come to hear of this talk.
So the church sent out Barnabas
All the way to Antioch.

11:23 When he arrived, he saw God's grace
And was glad it had been poured.
Then he urged all with a strong heart
To remain true to the Lord.

11:24 He was a good man, full of faith.
With God's[191] Spirit he was filled.
To the Lord there was then added
A great number *as God willed.

11:25 Then Barnabas left for Tarsus.
For Saul he made careful search.
11:26 When he found him, he brought him back
To Antioch's *now mixed church.

It came about for one whole year
That with the church they both met.
They taught great numbers of people.
Then a name for all was set.*

The disciples were called "Christians"
By outsiders in their talk.[192]
So this name originated
In the town of Antioch.

11:27 In those days from Jerusalem
To Antioch prophets came.
11:28 One of them stood before the church,
And Agabus was his name.

Through the Spirit he signified
That through all of Rome's domain[193]
A severe famine would occur,
Which took place in Claudius's reign.

11:29 The disciples then determined
(Those who had the means to share)
To send relief to Judea,
To the brothers living there.

11:30 And so they did, sending their gifts
To the elders who presided.
Through the hands of Barnabas and Saul
This relief was then provided.

12:1 About this time Herod the king,
Intending to persecute,
Laid his hands on some from the church,
12:2 And James he did execute.

This was James, the brother of John,
Whom by the sword he had killed.
12:3 Seeing that this had pleased the Jews,
To seize Peter he then willed.

In the days of Unleavened Bread,
The search for this apostle fell.
12:4 So when he had arrested him,
He put him in a prison cell.

He planned that after Passover
He'd bring him to public trial.
Herod had four squads of soldiers
Guard Peter in the meanwhile.

12:5 Therefore, Peter was being kept
In the prison by each squad,
But earnest prayers were being made
For him by the church to God.

12:6 The night before the day of court
That he was to be arraigned,
He was sleeping between two guards.
With two shackles he was chained.

The other two from the same squad
Were guarding the prison door.
12:7 An angel of the Lord appeared,
Standing on the prison floor.

Also a light shined in the cell
As the angel struck Peter's side
So as to rouse him from his sleep.
"Get up quickly," the angel cried.

The shackles fell off Peter's hands
12:8 As the angel instructed more,
"Put on your belt and your sandals."
This Peter did not ignore.

"Now wrap your cloak around yourself,
And follow me out," he said.
12:9 Peter went out and followed him,
Ignorant while being led.

For what the angel was doing
He did not know to be true
Because it simply seemed to be
A vision for him to view.

12:10 After passing two other guards,
They came to the iron gate
Which by itself opened for them.
To exit they did not wait.

The gate led into the city,
And after walking one street,
Immediately, the angel left,
The journey yet incomplete.*

12:11 When Peter came to his senses,
He said, "Now I understand.
The Lord has sent His angel out
To snatch me from Herod's hand.

"The Lord has sent His angel out
To dash the expectation
Of all the people of the Jews
Who wished my condemnation."*

12:12 When he realized that all was real,
He proceeded in the dark[194]
To the dwelling place of Mary,
The mother of John called Mark.

Many were gathered there for prayer
12:13 As on the gate's door he knocked.
A servant girl named Rhoda came
To answer, and she was shocked.

12:14 For she recognized Peter's voice.
Her joy she could not contain.
She ran back to give a report,
But it all sounded insane.

She left Peter standing out front,
Failing to open the gate.
"Peter's standing right out in front!"
She said in a joyful state.

12:15 "You are insane!" they all exclaimed,
But she persisted in her talk.
So they reasoned, "It's his angel."
12:16 And Peter continued to knock.

At last they opened up the door.
Seeing Peter, they were shocked;
12:17 Peter motioned with both his hands
To be silent as he talked.

He told them all just how the Lord
Walked him out the prison space.
He said, "Tell James and the brothers."
Then left for another place.

12:18 When daylight came, it was found out
By the soldiers in the cell
That Peter was no longer there,
And they both began to yell.

12:19 When Herod searched and found him not,
The guards he thoroughly drilled.
Unsatisfied by their answers,
He ordered them to be killed.

King Herod then went down from there,
The region of Judea,
Journeyed northward out to the coast,*
Staying in Caesarea.

12:20 Now with Tyre and Sidon's people
Herod was very displeased.
They came to him in one accord,
Blastus's aid having seized.

Blastus was the king's chamberlain,
For peace they through him pleaded
Since they secured from the king's land
Much of the food they needed.

12:21 Now on a day that had been fixed,
Herod clothed in kingly dress,
Began to give a public speech
On a throne to self express.

12:22 The audience kept crying out,
Herod's ego to applaud,*
"This is not the voice of a man.
It is the voice of a god!"

12:23 An angel of the Lord right then
Struck down Herod for his pride.
Since he failed to glorify God,
He was eaten by worms and died.

12:24 Now the Lord's word kept on growing.
It increased and multiplied,
12:25 And Barnabas and Saul returned
From bearing the gifts supplied.

They came back from Jerusalem,
Having fulfilled their mission.
With them was John, also called Mark,
Who was a new addition.*

13:1 Throughout the church at Antioch
Prophets and teachers arose.
Now here's a list of some of them.*
There were others, I suppose:[195]

Now first of all was Barnabas,
Named for his encouragement,
Originally known as Joseph,
A Cyprian by descent.[196]

There was Simeon, called Niger,
And Lucius from Cyrene;
Manaen, reared with King Herod,
And then Saul, whom we have seen.

13:2 While worshipping God and fasting,
The Holy Spirit declared,
"Set apart Saul and Barnabas
For the work I have prepared."

13:3 They obeyed the Holy Spirit,*
For upon them hands were laid.
The church sent them on their journey
After they fasted and prayed.

13:4 Thus sent by the Holy Spirit,
At Seleucia they hopped
On a ship and sailed to Cyprus.
13:5 Then at Salamis they stopped.

In the synagogues of the Jews
God's word they proclaimed and shared.
They also had Mark go with them
To help them as they declared.

13:6 They traveled across the island
Until to Paphos they came.
They found a certain Jewish man.
Bar-Jesus was the man's name.

Bar-Jesus was a sorcerer,
A false prophet full of guile.[197]
13:7 He was with Sergius Paulus,
A smart man who ruled the isle.

The ruler sought to hear God's word
And called Barnabas and Saul,
13:8 But the sorcerer opposed them
And began a verbal brawl.

Now Elymas means sorcerer,
And this Greek name he preferred.*
He wanted to turn the ruler
Away from faith in the word.

13:9 However, Saul, also called Paul,
Looked Elymas in the eye.
And filled with the Holy Spirit,
13:10 Paul gave him a firm reply.

"You are full of all kinds of things,
Full of trickery and guile.
You enemy of righteousness,
You're the devil's son! You're vile!

"When will you stop making crooked
The Lord's straight and truthful ways?
13:11 Behold, God's hand will strike you blind.
You won't see the sun for days."

Immediately mist and darkness
Fell on him, his sight denied.
Wandering about, he was groping
For someone to be his guide.

13:12 When the ruler had witnessed this
And all that had been achieved,
Fully awed by the Lord's teachings,
He, Sergius Paulus, believed.

13:13 Paul along with his companions
From Paphos put out to sea
To Perga in Pamphylia
With John in the company.

But while they were there in Perga,
John left and abandoned them.
He returned back to his home town,
Back home to Jerusalem.

13:14 From there they went to Antioch,
That is, the Pisidian town.
They went into the synagogue
On the Sabbath and sat down.

13:15 After some Scriptures had been read
From the Prophets and the Law,
The ruler of the synagogue
Sent for the guests whom he saw.

"Brothers, if you have any words
For the people, please address.
We would like to listen to you.
To the council you express."

13:16 After standing, Paul raised his hands,
"Men of Israel," he addressed,
"Also you who revere our God,
Listen to what I attest.

13:17 "The God of this people, Israel,
Chose our fathers and with His hand
Raised the people who were strangers
In the mighty Egyptian land.

"With a strong arm God led them out
13:18 Into the wilderness places,
But for a forty-year period,
He put up with their disgraces.

13:19 "And when in the land of Canaan
He overthrew seven nations,
He gave the land to our people.
By lot He made allocations.

13:20 "The next four hundred fifty years,
Judges to them God then brought
Until the prophet Samuel came,
13:21 After which a king they sought.

"After asking, God gave to them
The man Saul, the son of Kish,
Out of the tribe of Benjamin,
Fulfilling the people's wish.

"But after ruling forty years,
13:22 God removed Saul from the throne.
He raised up David as their king,
About whom He made this known:

"'I have found David, Jesse's son,
A man after My own heart.
He'll accomplish all of My will,
My whole will, not just one part.'*

13:23 "From the descendants of this man,
Fulfilling that promise of old,
He's brought a Savior to Israel.
13:24 He's Jesus, as John foretold.

"Before Jesus had come to us,
To the people John had preached
A baptism of repentance.
To all Israel this had reached.

13:25 "As John was completing his course,
He was saying, 'What's your thought?
Who do you think I really am,
The Messiah? I am not!

"'But there's One coming after me.
Behold, *He's the one to meet.
I am unworthy to remove
The sandals worn on His feet.'

13:26 "O men, brothers, Abraham's sons,
Also you who revere our God,
The message of this salvation
To us has been sent abroad.

13:27 "Those living in Jerusalem
And their rulers judged Him instead.
They did not know, though each Sabbath
They had heard the prophets read.

"By judging Him in ignorance,
The prophecies they fulfilled.
13:28 Although they found no grounds for death,
They asked Pilate that He be killed.

13:29 "When all that stands written of Him
Was completed by their aid,
They took Him down from off the tree,
And Him in a tomb they laid.

13:30 "But Him God raised up from the dead.
13:31 For many days, Him they did see,
They who had come up with Him
To Jerusalem from Galilee.

"These are those who to the people
Are His witnesses in this day.
13:32 So this good news, the gospel word,
To you all we now convey.

"The promise made to the fathers,
13:33 For their children God fulfilled,
Their children who are all of us.
Yes, it happened as God willed.*

"For God Himself raised up Jesus
As is written in Psalm Two:
'You Yourself are My very Son.
This day I've begotten You.'

13:34 "God raised Him up from the dead,
Never to go to decay.
As to this fact God has spoken
In the Scriptures in this way:

"'The holy and sure I'll give you,
David's blessings, *that is to say.'
13:35 Elsewhere He states, 'I won't allow
Your Holy One to see decay.'

13:36 "Now David, having by God's plan
Served his own generation,
Died, was buried with his fathers,
And saw deterioration.

13:37 "But He whom God resurrected
Did not undergo decay.
13:38 Men and brothers, let it be clear
What we're telling you this day.

“Through this One sins are forgiven
13:39 For those who in Him believe,
Who are justified from all things,
Which through Law[198] none could receive.

“Only by believing in Him
Does righteousness come to all.
13:40 Therefore, beware that what’s been said
In the Prophets on you won’t fall:

13:41 “‘Look scoffers, marvel and perish.
In your days this work I’ll do,
A work that you’ll never believe
Even if someone told you.’”

13:42 While the two men were exiting,
With them the crowd was pleading
To speak to them about these words
On the next Sabbath meeting.

13:43 When the synagogue was dismissed,
Some Jews, a number not small,
With many religious converts,
Followed Barnabas and Paul.

So then both Paul and Barnabas,
Not ceasing to speak their case,
Were encouraging all of them
To continue in God’s grace.

13:44 When the coming Sabbath arrived,
Into the meeting there poured
Almost the entire city
To hear the word of the Lord.

13:45 When the Jews saw the multitudes,
With jealousy they were filled.
They were opposing Paul's preaching.
Evil words from their lips spilled.

13:46 Paul and Barnabas boldly said,
"It was urgent that we speak
The word of God to you Jews first,
But God's word you do not seek.

"Since you rejected what we've said,
And yourselves you deem unfit,
Unworthy of eternal life,
To the Gentiles we'll offer it.

13:47 "For thus the Lord has ordered us,
'I've placed you for every nation
As a light so that you might bring
To the earth's ends salvation.'"

13:48 Hearing this, the Gentiles rejoiced.
God's word they praised and received.
Everyone who had been ordained
To eternal life believed.

13:49 Throughout that land the Lord's word spread.
13:50 So the Jews brought a committee
Of devout, respected women
And of leaders of the city.

They stirred up a persecution
Against Barnabas and Paul,
Driving them out of the region,
13:51 And dust from the feet did fall.

Paul and Barnabas shook their feet
In protest against all this.
13:52 They went to Iconium filled
With God's Spirit and with bliss.

14:1 Later, while in Iconium,
As was their custom to do,
They entered the Jewish synagogue
To speak to the Greek and Jew.

They spoke in a certain manner
So that a large number believed.
Not only did the Jewish crowd,
But the word, Greeks too received.

14:2 Now those Jews who did not believe
Used strategies of all kinds
To stir up against these brothers
Gentiles by tainting their minds.

14:3 So therefore, Paul and Barnabas
Stayed a long time in that place,
Having great courage in the Lord
Who affirmed the word of His grace.

The Lord did so by giving them
The ability to do
Both signs and wonders by their hands,
14:4 Which split the town into two.

For some of them aligned themselves
With the unbelieving Jews.
While all the others in the town,
The apostles they did choose.

14:5 Eventually, a plot arose
To attack and have them stoned.
Gentiles and Jews with their rulers,
This strategy they condoned.

14:6 Paul and Barnabas, learning this,
From Iconium ran out
To Lycaonia, Lystra,
Derbe, and the region about.

14:7 While they were there in those places,
They continued with their mission
By proclaiming the gospel news
To everyone who would listen.

14:8 While at Lystra, there sat this man
Who could not stand on his feet.
He was never able to walk,
Born crippled *and incomplete.

14:9 Paul saw this man's faith to be healed
Who listened as he was talking.
14:10 Paul eyed him and yelled, "On your feet!"
He began leaping and walking!

14:11 Seeing Paul's deed, the crowd then yelled
In the Lycaonian tongue,
"In the likeness of human men
Upon us the gods have sprung!"

14:12 They were calling Barnabas, Zeus.
Paul was Hermes in their view,
For they considered Paul to be
The chief speaker of the two.

14:13 Now just outside the city gates
The temple of Zeus stood tall.
This was where the lame man had begged,*
And where he was healed by Paul.*

The priest of Zeus brought bulls and wreaths
To the city's entrance way.
He was wanting, with all the crowds,
To slaughter the bulls that day.

14:14 When the apostles heard this plan,
They shouted extremely loud.
Paul and Baranabas tore their robes
And rushed out into the crowd.

14:15 They said, "We're mortals just like you!
Men, why plan such insanity?
We proclaim the good news to you
To turn you from this vanity.

"Turn to the God who is living,
The only God we proclaim,*
Who made the heavens and the earth,
The sea and all they contain.

14:16 "In previous generations
All the nations God let go
To live however they wanted,
14:17 But left evidence below.

"For God did good. He gave you rains
From His heavenly creation,
Fruitful seasons, filling your hearts
With food and jubilation."

14:18 Even after saying these things,
They almost could not prevent
The crowds from slaying bulls to them.
But finally they did consent.

14:19 Now Jews came from Iconium,
And also from Antioch,
Winning over the multitudes
To not listen to Paul's talk.*

So after throwing stones at Paul,
Assuming that he had died,
They dragged him out of the city
And left him for dead outside.

14:20 As the disciples stood around,
Paul got up and walked away,
Entered town, but left for Derbe
With Barnabas on the next day.

14:21 After they had preached the gospel
To Derbe's population
And had made many disciples,
They returned as motivation.

They went through the towns of Lystra,
Iconium, and Antioch,
14:22 Strengthening the disciples' souls
To live in the Christian walk.[199]

They told them that tribulations*
They were not to think as odd,*
"We, through many tribulations,
Must enter the kingdom of God."

14:23 Now for each church they chose elders,
And this with fasting and praying.
They entrusted them to the Lord
In whom their faith had been staying.

14:24 Then they passed through Pisidia,
But in Pamphylia they stopped.
14:25 Once they preached the word in Perga,
To Attalia they dropped.

14:26 From there they sailed to Antioch
Where they had been commended
To the grace of God for this work,
Which work they now had ended.

14:27 When they arrived at Antioch,
They gathered the church and reviewed
Everything God had done with them,
And that Gentiles He did include.

They told them how a door of faith,
God opened for the Gentile.
14:28 So they stayed with the disciples
In Antioch for quite a while.

15:1 Some men came down from Judea
And were teaching the brothers this:
"Be circumcised as Moses said,
Or salvation you will miss."

15:2 Such great debate and sharp disputes
From Paul and Barnabas came,
That the brothers told them to go
To Jerusalem's domain.

A group with Paul and Barnabas,
To Jerusalem were sent
To the apostles and elders
To resolve this argument.

15:3 Therefore, being sent by the church,
Through Phoenicia they passed.
Then they went through Samaria,
And great joy their presence cast.

For everywhere believers were
In great detail they explained
The conversion of the Gentiles,
Which produced joy unrestrained.

15:4 Arriving at Jerusalem,
They all were welcomed by these:
By the apostles and elders,
And by the church attendees.

They told them all God did with them,
15:5 But some stood up to object.
They were a group of believers
Out of the Pharisee's sect.

"You must have them all circumcised,"
The faction began to compel,
"And you must command them to keep
The Law of Moses as well."

15:6 The apostles and the elders
Were assembled in one place
To analyze this dialogue
Concerning the Law and grace.*

15:7 After there had been much debate,
Peter stood and to them said,
"Men, brothers, you already know
Early on how I was led.

"You know that among you God chose
That through the words from my jaws
The Gentiles should hear the good news
And believe *without Jewish laws.

15:8 "God is the knower of the heart
And proved that they were not lost.
He gave them the Holy Spirit
As He gave us at Pentecost.[200]

15:9 "And so between Jews and Gentiles
God made no distinction, none,
Because He cleansed their hearts by faith
As they trusted in God's Son.*

15:10 "So why place a yoke on their necks?
Why now put God to the test?
For by this unbearable yoke
Our fathers and we have been pressed.

15:11 "But we believe salvation comes
Through the grace of Jesus our Lord;
So in the same way these were saved."
15:12 Silence upon the crowd poured.

Then Barnabas and Paul explained
(The crowd listening to these men)
All the signs and wonders God did
Among the Gentiles through them.

15:13 After they had finished speaking,
James responded with this speech:
"Men and brothers, listen to me.
A conclusion I now will reach.*

15:14 "Simon has explained to us all
God's first visit to obtain
From among the Gentile nations
A people for His own name.

15:15 "The Prophets' words agree with this
As is written to be fulfilled,
15:16 'After these things I will return.
David's tent I will rebuild.

"'For David's tent has fallen down,
And it will be redesigned.
I'll rebuild, restore its ruins
15:17 For the sake of all mankind.

"'It's so that they will seek the Lord,
People from every nation,
All those that call upon My name,
15:18 Declares the Lord of salvation.

"'The Lord who is doing these things
Has already made it known
In the Scriptures of long ago.'
Now to us it has been shown.*

15:19 "Therefore, I now give my judgment.
For those who have turned to God
From the nations of the Gentiles,
More hardships we won't applaud.

15:20 "Instead let's write them to abstain
From idol contamination,
From foods strangled or filled with blood,
And from all fornication.

15:21 "For from early generations
In each city this was said
As Moses in the synagogues
Each Sabbath was preached and read."

15:22 So it seemed good to choose some men
To go with Barnabas and Paul
Back to the church in Antioch.
This action seemed good to all.

All apostles agreed to this.
The elders gave their okay.
The whole church consented to this,
To the selection that day.

They chose some men from among them,
Leaders among the brothers,
Judas who was called Barsabbas,
And Silas, *these two, no others.

15:23 They wrote this letter by their hand
To be read in the church meetings:[201]
"The apostles and the elders,
Your brothers, send you greetings.

"Yes, we greet you Gentile brothers
In the cities of Antioch,
Syria, and Cilicia,
To clear up how you must walk.*

15:24 "Some from us troubled you with words,
Of which we have been apprised,
Unsettling your very souls,
But they were unauthorized.

15:25 "We deemed it good to choose some men,
Having come to one accord,
To send with Paul and Barnabas
15:26 Who've risked their lives for the Lord.

"Paul and Barnabas risked it all
For our Lord Jesus Christ's name.
15:27 We send you Judas and Silas
To confirm by mouth the same.

15:28 "It seemed to the Holy Spirit
And to us that it was best
To place on you no added weight,
Save this essential request:

15:29 "That you abstain from all these things:
From idol contamination,
From foods strangled or filled with blood,
And from all fornication.

"For if you truly heed these words,
In your walk you will excel.
That's all we need to write to you.
We now bid you all farewell."

15:30 Therefore, they went to Antioch
Right after their dismissal.
They gathered the church together
And gave them this epistle.

15:31 Now after they finished reading
The epistle that had been sent,
The church was full of rejoicing
For all its encouragement.

15:32 Since Judas and Silas also
Were themselves a prophetic pair,
With many words they encouraged
And strengthened the brothers there.

15:33 After spending a span of time,
In peace they were sent away
By this church to those who sent them,
15:35 But the other two chose to stay.[202]

Paul and Barnabas chose to stay
In Antioch to give by speech
The Lord's word, with many others.
So they stayed to teach and preach.

15:36 Now after certain days had passed,
Paul to Barnabas proposed,
"Let's go and visit the brothers
To whom God's word was disclosed.

"Let's go to each and every town
We've preached the Lord's word so far
So that we may see these brothers
And find out just how they are."

15:37 Now Barnabas was arranging
To take John, also called Mark,
Along with them on this journey,
15:38 But discord began to spark.

Paul deemed it best not to take Mark
Since his duties he came to shirk,
Defecting from Pamphylia,
Not staying with them in the work.

15:39 Soon the discord became so sharp
They separated that day.
So Barnabas took Mark with him
And to Cyprus sailed away.

15:40 But Paul, after choosing Silas,
And then being commended
By the brothers to the Lord's grace,
Returned as he intended.

15:41 Through Syria and Cilicia
He returned, taking the time
To stop and strengthen every church,
Making sure that they were fine.*

16:1 He traveled also to Derbe,
Then to Lystra where he found
A disciple named Timothy
Who was staying in that town.

He was the son of this woman
Who was a believing Jew.
His father was of Greek descent,
And this fact the public knew.[203]

16:2 The Christian brothers everywhere,
Only good of him they'd tell,
Not just the brothers at Lystra,
But Iconium as well.

16:3 Paul wanted him to come with him,
But because the Jews well knew
His father was of Greek descent,
He circumcised this *half-Jew.

16:4 Then they all went throughout the towns,
Delivering the laws to heed
That the apostles and elders
At Jerusalem had decreed.

16:5 So in the faith the churches were
Being strengthened through and through,
And each and every single day
Were growing in numbers too.

16:6 And they traveled through the region,
Of Phrygia and Galatia,
Restrained by the Holy Spirit
From speaking the word in Asia.

16:7 Coming to Mysia's border,
They were trying to advance
Into Bithynia's region,
16:8 But they did not have the chance.

For the Spirit of Jesus Christ,
Their progress He did prevent.
So passing along Mysia,
Down to Troas they then went.

16:9 Paul saw a Macedonian
In a night vision he had seen
Who was standing and begging him
To come over and intervene.

"Please come to Macedonia
And help us," was how he pled.
16:10 After Paul saw the night vision,
He acted on what he said.

At once we sought to depart there,
Concluding God made the call
For us to preach the gospel there
And had made it clear to Paul.*

16:11 So from Troas to Samothrace
We set a straight course through the sea.
Next we sailed to Neapolis,
16:12 Then traveled to a colony.

This colony was Philippi,
A city that was foremost
In Eastern Macedonia,
About ten miles from the coast.*

We were staying here many days.
16:13 Then the Sabbath day arrived.
We went outside the city gate
To where we thought prayers thrived.

It was along the riverbank
That some women gathered to pray.
Sitting down with their assembly,
We were speaking to them that day.

16:14 One woman there, named Lydia,
Was a merchant from abroad,
From the city, Thyatira,
And a worshipper of God.

This merchant of purple fabrics
Was listening to us all.
Then the Lord opened up her heart
To heed what was spoken by Paul.

16:15 She and her household were baptized.
"Come and stay at my house," she pressed,
"Since you've deemed me faithful to God."
So we accepted her request.

16:16 After some time while on our way
To the place of prayer again,
We were met by a servant girl
Who had a spirit within.

This spirit, a demonic one,
The future through her revealed.
As a result for her masters
Lavish profits she would yield.

16:17 Tagging along with Paul and us,
She was crying out as she jawed,
"These who tell us salvation's way
Are servants of the Most High God."

16:18 She was doing this many days.
Then Paul being greatly perturbed,
Turned around and gave a command
To the spirit who him disturbed.

"I, in the name of Jesus Christ,
Command you from her to go!"
The very moment of these words,
The demon in her did so.

16:19 Now when her masters discovered
That their hope of gain was no more,
They captured both Paul and Silas,
The judges to bring them before.

They dragged them to the marketplace
16:20 Before the chief magistrates,
Saying, "Because these men are Jews,
Great disturbance this creates.

"They put our town into chaos,
16:21 Teaching customs we can't allow,
Things we can't receive nor observe,
Things we Romans must disavow."

16:22 Then against both Paul and Silas,
The crowd joined in verbal attacks.
The chief magistrates tore the robes
Off Paul's and Silas's backs.

They ordered that they be beaten,
16:23 And after many stripes befell,
They threw them into jail then charged
The jailor to guard them well.

16:24 Since he received this kind of charge,
He put them in the inner cell
And fastened their feet in the stocks.
The jailor was guarding them well.*

16:25 About midnight Paul and Silas,
While praying and petitioning,
Were singing melodies to God.
The prisoners were listening.

16:26 Suddenly, a huge quake occurred,
Shaking the jail's foundations.
At once, all doors flew wide open.
Chains fell off in all locations.

16:27 When the jailor woke up and saw
All the jail doors opened wide,
Thinking the prisoners had escaped,
He drew the sword from his side.

He was about to kill himself,
16:28 But Paul spoke up with a shout,
"Do not do this harm to yourself,
For we're here; not one is out!"

16:29 Calling for lights, he ran inside,
And with fear and great alarm
Fell down before Paul and Silas,
16:30 Then led them out by the arm.

He said to them, "Sirs, please tell me,
To be saved what must I do?"
16:31 "Believe upon the Lord Jesus,
And you'll be saved," said the two.

"This good news is not just for you
But all in your house who dwell."
16:32 So they spoke the Lord's word to him
And to all his household as well.

16:33 That very hour of the night
He washed all their wounds with care.
Immediately, he was baptized,
Also all his household there.

16:34 The jailor brought them to his home
And set food before their face.
He rejoiced with all the household,
Having trusted in God's grace.[204]

16:35 When it was light, the magistrates
Sent to the jail their police.
They gave to them orders, saying,
"Those two men you must release."

16:36 Then the jailor told Paul these words,
"I have orders for your release.
The magistrates have ordered this.
So depart and leave in peace."

16:37 Paul said to them, "Without a trial
They've beaten us with a whip
Although we are men who possess
The Roman citizenship.

"They did this in the public's eye,
And then into jail we were thrust.
Now they want a secret release?
No! Escort us out, they must!"

16:38 The police told the magistrates
What to them had been made known.
The magistrates feared when they heard
That they were citizens of Rome.

16:39 So coming, they appealed to them
And escorted them out of there.
Wanting them to leave the city,
They were begging this from the pair.

16:40 From the jail they went to the home
Of Lydia to say good-bye,
Saw the brothers, encouraged them,
Then exited Philippi.

17:1 They traveled through Amphipolis
On the roadway used for trade,[205]
Then went through Apollonia,
But in the next town they stayed.

Thessalonica was this town
Where there was a synagogue
In which the Jewish people met
To learn and to dialogue.*

17:2 Paul went to those assembled there
In his customary ways.
From the Scriptures he challenged them
For the next three Sabbath days.

17:3 He was explaining and proving,
From what the prophets had said,
That the Christ would have to suffer
And rise again from the dead.

Then he told them about Jesus
And concluded with this news,
"This Jesus I proclaim to you,
Is Christ, *the King of the Jews."

17:4 Of those persuaded, some were Jews,
A mass were God-fearing Greeks,
And many were leading women
In the course of those three weeks.[206]

17:5 As this crowd joined Paul and Silas,
Envy filled the other Jews
Who went into the marketplace
Seeking evil men to choose.

They took these men and formed a mob.
Into chaos the town was thrown.
Wanting the preachers to appear,
They rushed against Jason's home.

17:6 But when they could not find the men,
Jason and some brothers they caught,
Dragged them to the city rulers
As accusations they brought.

"Two men who've upset all the world
Have come here into our town;
17:7 Jason received them as his guest.
These all oppose Caesar's crown.

"They practice things that are against
The decrees of Caesar's reign,
Saying there is another king
And that Jesus is His name."

17:8 Now both the crowd and the rulers
Were stirred up by this report.
17:9 Jason was released with the rest
When they paid bond to the court.

17:10 The brothers sent Paul and Silas
To Berea on that night,
Who went to the Jewish synagogue
When arriving at that site.

17:11 The Bereans were more noble
Than Thessalonica's Jews,
For when the word was being preached,
To listen they did not refuse.

They eagerly received the word
And searched the Scriptures each day,
Making sure that what they had heard
Was what the Scriptures did say.

17:12 Therefore, many of them believed,
And some of the Greeks did too,
Well-respected women and men.
And their numbers were not few.

17:13 When the Thessalonian Jews
Heard Paul was preaching God's word,
They came to the Berean crowds
Whom they unsettled and stirred.

17:14 At once the brothers sent Paul off
To the sea *some miles away,
But both Silas and Timothy
Were left in Berea to stay.

17:15 An escort led Paul to Athens.
Then with orders were sent away
To tell Silas and Timothy
To join Paul without delay.

17:16 Now while Paul was waiting for them,
His inner spirit was annoyed
As he saw idols everywhere
Which all the city enjoyed.*

17:17 So he spoke in the synagogue
With godly Greeks and the Jews,
And daily in the marketplace
With those who would hear his views.

17:18 Epicureans and Stoics
Were debating with him one day.
Some of these philosophers sneered,
"What's this babbler wish to say?"

"It seems that he is proclaiming
A foreign god," others said,
Since he was preaching the good news
Of Jesus risen from the dead.

17:19 So they brought him to the meeting,
Known as the Areopagus.
"We wish to know this new teaching
Which you are proclaiming to us.

17:20 "For you are bringing strange concepts
Which our ears have never heard.
Therefore, we plan to discover
What you mean by this new word."

17:21 (Now the strangers visiting there,
And all Athenians too,
Spent all their time either talking
Or listening to something new.)

17:22 In the midst of the Areopagus
Paul stood and began to say:
"Men of Athens, I see you are
Very pious in every way.

17:23 "For while roaming through and noting
Your worship objects as shown,
I found an altar with these words:
'To the God who is unknown.'

"Therefore, the One whom you don't know,
Whom you strive to worship too,
This is the One that I myself
Will right now proclaim to you.

17:24 "The God who made this world of ours
And all things within its confines,
Since He's Lord of heaven and earth,
Does not live in man-made shrines.

17:25 "Nor is He served by human hands,
For He never is in need
Since He gives to all life and breath
And everything else, indeed.

17:26 "From one He made all ethnic groups
Upon the earth's face to dwell,
Establishing their rise and fall
And all their boundaries as well.

17:27 “This was so they’d seek after God
If Him they’d just grope and find,
Though He’s not very far from us
Or from any of mankind.[207]

17:28 “For in Him we live, move, and are.
With this your poets have agreed.[208]
For some of them have written this:
‘For we are His offspring, indeed.’

17:29 “Therefore, as the offspring of God,
We must not put in our mind
That the divine nature is like
Something that man has designed.

“We must not think that He is like,
Stone idols, silver, or gold,
Reflections of the thoughts of man,
Fashioned from a human mold.

17:30 “For although man’s past ignorance
To look past God did consent,
He is commanding everywhere
That everyone must repent.

17:31 “For He has fixed a day on which
He’ll judge all those of this earth
In a man whom He appointed
Who has proved His place of worth.*

“God has given sufficient proof
To all concerning this fact
By raising Him up from the dead
With evidence of that act.”*

17:32 This concept of raising the dead
Caused some to scoff at Paul's word,
But others said, "Another time
Tell us more of what we've heard."

17:33 At this Paul left from their presence,
17:34 But some men chose to unite,
Among whom was Dionysius
Who was an Areopagite.

A woman, known as Damaris,
To Paul's party also cleaved.
And there were others too who joined.
All joined because they believed.

18:1 After these things Paul left Athens.
He came to Corinth and found
18:2 A certain Jew born in Pontus
Who recently moved to town.

For Claudius had commanded
All the Jews to leave from Rome.
Therefore, this Jew named Aquila,
With his wife Priscilla left home.

18:3 Paul went to them and worked with them
Because they shared the same trade.
They worked together making tents,
And with this couple Paul stayed.

18:4 On each and every Sabbath day
He went to the synagogue,
Tried to persuade both Jews and Greeks,
Engaging in dialogue.

18:5 But when from Macedonia
Silas and Timothy came,
Paul exclusively preached the word,
And from his trade did abstain.[209]

He testified to all the Jews
That the Christ was Jesus who came,
18:6 But when they opposed and blasphemed,
He shook out his clothes in disdain.

"Your own blood be upon your heads.
I am clean," to them Paul said.
"From this time on I will proceed
To the Gentile world instead."

18:7 Leaving from there, he went next door
To Titius Justus's home.
This man worshipped the one true God,
Although a Gentile of Rome.[210]

18:8 The ruler of the synagogue,
Or Crispus as he was known,
Came to believe, trusting the Lord
With everyone in his home.

Many of the Corinthians
Who heard what Paul had to say
Believed his word, and trusted Christ,
And were baptized right away.

18:9 In a vision during the night,
The Lord spoke these words to Paul,
"Don't be fearful. Keep on speaking.
Don't become silent at all.

18:10 "No one will attack you with harm.
I am with you, so be brave,
For in this Corinthian town
I have many yet to save."

18:11 So he stayed there for eighteen months
Among them teaching God's word.
18:12 One day a united attack
On Paul by the Jews occurred.

Now Gallio was the ruler
Of Achaia at that time.
The Jews grabbed Paul and brought him to
The judgment seat to malign.

18:13 "This man is persuading people
To worship God the wrong way,
In a manner that contradicts
Our Law," they began to say.

18:14 Paul was about to speak some words,
But Gallio said to the Jews,
"If it's a wrong or evil crime,
I'd have reason to hear your views.

18:15 "Since it concerns some word or names
According to your Law, O Jews,
Settle all that among yourselves!
To judge such things, I refuse."

18:16 So Gallio drove them away
From the step of the judgment seat.
18:17 The ruler of the synagogue,
The Jews seized and began to beat.

The ruler's name was Sosthenes,
Whom they beat before the court.
Gallio displayed no concern.
Their action he did not thwart.*

18:18 Now Paul remained many more days
Before leaving the brothers there.
He was sailing to Syria
Without any head of hair.

For while he was in Cenchrea,
He shaved his head for a vow.
Priscilla and Aquila too
Accompanied Paul for now.

18:19 After coming to Ephesus,
Paul left the couple behind.
He went into the synagogue
And addressed his Jewish kind.

18:20 They wished that he'd remain longer.
Their plea he did not receive
18:21 But said farewell to all of them,
Pledging as he went to leave.

"I will return again to you
When God wills this to be."
Then he set sail from Ephesus
And journeyed across the sea.[211]

18:22 He landed at Caesarea
And went up to greet the flock[212]
Assembled in Jerusalem,
Then went down to Antioch.

18:23 After some time in Antioch
With the brothers Paul had spent,
He left from there strategically.*
On a third mission trip he went.*

Through the region of Galatia,
Then of Phrygia Paul paced,
Stopping in the towns to strengthen
All disciples that he faced.

18:24 Meanwhile some Jew named Apollos
At Ephesus had arrived,
An Alexandrian by birth
Who in education thrived.

In the Scriptures he was mighty,
18:25 Having been taught the Lord's way.
Being fervent in his spirit,
Things of Jesus he'd convey.

Although the things about Jesus
He was teaching accurately,
He was only familiar with
The baptism of John, you see.

18:26 As he began to boldly speak
In the Jewish synagogue,
Priscilla and Aquila heard
And had private dialogue.

For they explained to him God's way
More accurate and concrete
Since his knowledge about Jesus,*
Although right, was incomplete.*

18:27 When Apollos wanted to go
To Achaia across the sea,
The brothers wrote the disciples
To welcome him eagerly.

After coming, he greatly helped
Those who had believed through grace.
18:28 For he mightily refuted
The Jews in a public place.

He showed the Jews from the Scriptures,
In a way that surely sufficed,
The identity of Jesus,
That He had to be the Christ.

19:1 Sometime later while Apollos
Was in Corinth touching hearts,[213]
Paul arrived back at Ephesus,
Passing through the upper parts.

Certain disciples he found there
19:2 And asked them, "Did you receive
The Holy Spirit of the Lord
After you came to believe?"

They said to him, "No, we have not.
About Him we've never heard.
Just who this Holy Spirit is
We've never been told a word."

19:3 "What baptism did you receive?"
Paul questioned the group of men.
"John's baptism," was their reply.
19:4 Therefore, Paul explained to them.

"John baptized with a baptism
That required one to repent,
Telling the people to believe
On the One who would be sent.

"This person would come after him,
And Jesus is this One's name.
Repent and place your faith in Him,*
This One who already came."*

19:5 After hearing, they were baptized
Into Jesus's name, the Lord,
19:6 And when Paul laid his hands on them,
The Spirit on them was poured.

They were speaking in unknown tongues.
Prophecies from them did flow.
19:7 The total number in this group
Amounted to twelve men or so.

19:8 The next three months Paul boldly preached
As he entered the synagogue,
Telling the things of God's kingdom
In persuasive dialogue.

19:9 But certain ones were growing hard,
Were refusing to obey.
These openly before the crowd
Spoke evil about the Way.

Therefore, Paul took the disciples
And abandoned the synagogue.
He in the school of Tyrannus
Engaged daily in dialogue.

19:10 This continued for two more years
So that all in Asia heard
(Including both the Jews and Greeks)
The preaching of the Lord's word.

19:11 Now God was working miracles
Which were not common at all,
Extraordinary wonders
By means of the hands of Paul.

19:12 Even aprons and handkerchiefs
That came from the skin of Paul
And touched the sick and demon-possessed
Brought healing to them all.

19:13 Now certain Jewish exorcists
Who were traveling all around
Attempted to use Jesus's name
On those who by demons were bound.

To the evil spirits they'd say,
"In this name we now adjure,
The name Jesus, whom Paul preaches,"
Thinking success they'd procure.*

19:14 There were seven sons of Sceva,
Who was a Jewish chief priest,
That were using this formula
To get a demon released.

19:15 An evil spirit answered them,
"Of Jesus I'm well aware,
And as for Paul, I understand,
But who are you to declare?"

19:16 Then the man jumped on the seven
With the evil spirit inside.
He overpowered all of them
With beatings fiercely applied.

So relentless were the beatings
That it shredded all their clothes.
They ran out of the house naked
And injured from all the blows.

19:17 All those living in Ephesus
Came to learn about this news.
Fear fell on every one of them,
On both the Greeks and the Jews.

So the name of the Lord Jesus
Was being held up in respect.
19:18 Many believers were coming,
Convicted of their neglect.*

They were confessing openly
Their practices that were wrong.
19:19 Many who practiced magic arts
Brought their magic books along.

They put all their books in a pile
And burned them before all eyes.
Fifty thousand silver pieces
Was the worth of these supplies.

19:20 In this way the word of the Lord
Was growing and waxing strong.
19:21 Then after all this had occurred,
Paul resolved to move along.

To travel to Jerusalem,
In the Spirit Paul set his heart.
But first for Macedonia
And Achaia he would depart.

His traveling itinerary*
To all he was making known,*
Saying, "After Jerusalem,
I must also visit Rome."

19:22 Paul sent to Macedonia
Two of those serving him fine
Named Timothy and Erastus.
So in Asia he spent more time.

19:23 It happened that about this time
In matters about the Way,
Great commotion began to stir
By what craftsmen would convey.*

19:24 It started with a certain man.
Demetrius was his name.
He was by trade a silversmith,
Bringing many no small gain.

The silver shrines of Artemis
Was the product that he made,
Employing many artisans
In the much-demanded trade.

19:25 He organized a great meeting
Of those in his vocation
Along with other artisans
Of similar occupation.

He said, "O men, you know too well
That our wealth comes from this trade.
19:26 Paul is saying that they aren't gods
Which by our hands have been made.

"You see and hear in Ephesus
And throughout Asia, nearly,
Paul persuading great crowds to turn,
19:27 Costing our business dearly.

"Not just our trade is in danger
Of coming to disrespect,
But the temple of Artemis
This will adversely affect.

"For the great goddess Artemis
Who is worshipped and enjoyed
By all of Asia and this world,
Her greatness will be destroyed."

19:28 The people there were filled with rage
As they listened to these reasons.
They were all shouting, "Great she is,
Artemis of the Ephesians."

19:29 The whole city being caught up
In the tumultuous pride,
Forced Gaius and Aristarchus
To the theatre's inside.

These men from Macedonia
Would travel with Paul to and fro.
19:30 Paul planned to go into that crowd,
But the disciples told him, "No!"

19:31 Some leading Asian officials,
Who had become friends of Paul,
Sent word that he not put himself
In the theatre at all.

19:32 Some people were shouting one thing.
Something else others would blare.
For most of the assembled crowd
Did not know why they were there.

19:33 From the crowd Alexander rose,
The Jews pushing him to stand.
He was wanting to build a case
As he motioned them with his hand.

19:34 Because they saw he was a Jew,
And for no other reasons,*
They yelled for two hours, "Great she is,
Artemis of the Ephesians."

19:35 Then the town clerk silenced the crowd,
"Ephesian men, quiet down!
What people out there do not know
The customs of this great town?

"This town is the temple keeper
Over Artemis the Great
As well as over her image
Which fell from heaven's estate.

19:36 "Since this is without argument,
Undeniably the facts,
You must all remain orderly
And refrain from hasty acts.

19:37 "For these two men, which you have brought,
Did not from our temple steal,
Nor our goddess did they blaspheme.
So terminate this ordeal.*

19:38 "Now therefore, if Demetrius
And those with him in his trade
Have any word against someone,
Their charges can now be made.

"For the courts are now in session.
The proconsuls are at hand.
Let all charges against others
Be brought this way, understand.

19:39 "And if you seek something further,
It will be settled one way,
In an assembly that's legal,
19:40 Unlike the gathering today.[214]

"For we're in danger of the charge
Of causing today's discord.
We've no answer for the uproar.
No cause can be underscored."

19:41 After everything had been said
By the town clerk on that day,
He ordered that the assembly
Be dismissed and on their way.

20:1 When the uproar came to a halt,
For the disciples Paul sent.
He encouraged them, said farewell,
Then to Macedonia went.

20:2 Exhorting many in those parts
By the many words conveyed,
He finally ended up in Greece
20:3 Where for three whole months he stayed.

Ready to sail to Syria,
A Jewish assault plan was learned.
Paul, deciding to change his course,
Through Macedonia returned.

20:4 Paul was being accompanied
By these who are of renown:[215]
Sopater the son of Pyrrhus,
From the noble Berean town;

Aristarchus and Secundus,
Who were from not far from there.
The town of Thessalonica
Was the home town of this pair;

Gaius, who had come from Derbe;
Timothy, who proved his worth;
And Tychicus with Trophimus,
Who in Asia had their birth.

20:5 These men went ahead to Troas,
Waiting for us to come by.
20:6 After the Feast of Unleavened Bread,
We sailed from Philippi.

It took us five days to get there,
But in Troas them we found.
Seven more days we tarried there,
Deciding to stick around.*

20:7 Now on the first day of the week
We had been sharing a meal.
Paul, intending to leave at day,
Began to talk a great deal.

He preached to them until midnight,
20:8 But the darkness did not bloom,
For many lights were at that place
Which was in an upper room.

20:9 Sitting upon the windowsill
Was a young man fighting sleep.
This young man's name was Eutychus.
He fell in a slumber deep.

As Paul was talking on and on,
He fell off the windowsill,
Down three stories onto the ground,
And him the impact did kill.*

He was dead when they picked him up,
20:10 But Paul ran down in a hurry.
Falling on him and holding him,
He said, "Stop all of your worry!

"For his life is now within him!"
20:11 Then Paul went up to the room.
After breaking bread and eating,
His address he did resume.

He picked up right where he left off,
Addressing them through the night.
He talked until the crack of dawn
Then departed from their sight.

20:12 They took from there the youth alive,
Comforted without measure.
20:13 And we set sail ahead of Paul,
For to walk was his good pleasure.

We boarded a ship to Assos.
Paul walked as was his intent.
20:14 There we took him onto the ship,
And to Mitylene we went.

20:15 The second day we sailed from there,
About fifty miles we spanned.*
We anchored opposite Chios,
Not bothering to go on land.[216]

The third day we came to Samos.
To Miletus on the fourth day,
20:16 For Paul had planned to sail on by
Ephesus to avoid delay.

His rush was to Jerusalem.
In Asia no time could be lost.
He wished, if likely, to arrive
For the day of Pentecost.

20:17 So Paul arranged from Miletus
A final farewell oration[217]
To the Ephesian church elders,
Whom he called to his location.

20:18 When they arrived he said to them,
"You all are very aware,
From the time I stepped in Asia,
I was always with you there.

20:19 "You know just how I served the Lord
With all humbleness and tears
Through the trials that came on me
In the Jewish plots those years.

20:20 "I withheld nothing good from you,
But to you made all things known,
Preaching and teaching publicly,
As well as from home to home.

20:21 "Both to the Jews and to the Greeks
I testified and implored
To turn to God in repentance
And trust in Jesus, our Lord.

20:22 "To go now to Jerusalem
By the Spirit I'm compelled,
And what things will befall me there,
That knowledge has been withheld.

20:23 "I just know the Holy Spirit
In each town has testified
That both chains and tribulations
On me will one day abide.

20:24 "But I don't count my very life
As precious to me at all
In order that I might complete
My course and service, God's call.

"I received from the Lord Jesus
This life course and ministry
To testify of the good news
Of the grace of God that's free.

20:25 "And now I know that none of you
Among whom I went before,
Proclaiming the kingdom of God,
Will see my face anymore.

20:26 "So I declare this day, I'm clean
From the blood of every man,
20:27 For I shunned not to tell to you
All of God's counsel, God's plan.

20:28 “Watch yourselves and all of the flock
Over which you’ve been ordained.
By the Holy Spirit of God
As overseers you’ve been named.

“You must shepherd the church of God
Whom He bought with His own blood,
20:29 For I know, after I depart,
That wolves among you will flood.

“These savage wolves won’t spare the flock.
20:30 From you will arise such men
Who’ll speak wrong things to draw away
The disciples after them.

20:31 “So keep alert, bearing in mind
That for the space of three years
I ceased not warning each of you
Nightly and daily with tears.

20:32 “I now entrust you all to God
And to the word of His grace,
Which is able to build you up
And give you a secure place.*

“This gift is an inheritance
Among all the sanctified.
20:33 No one’s silver, gold, or clothing,
Have I coveted or eyed.

20:34 “You yourselves know that with these hands
I worked to meet my own needs
And of those accompanying me,
Which you’ve witnessed by my deeds.*

20:35 "In every way I've shown you that
By toil we must help the weak,
Bearing in mind these famous words
Which now to you I will speak.*

"Our Lord Jesus has told to us
This beatitude to believe:*
'It's more blessed for you to give
Than it is for you to receive.'"

20:36 Then after he had said these things,
He knelt and prayed with them all.
20:37 Tears flowed as they kissed him farewell,
As they hugged the neck of Paul.

20:38 But most of all, by this report
They were extremely distraught,
That they would see his face no more.
Yet him to the boat they brought.

21:1 Later after parting from them
To set sail and get underway,
We came to Cos by a straight route,
Then to Rhodes the very next day.

From there we came to Patara,
21:2 Where a ship that we unveiled
Was to cross to Phoenicia.
So we boarded it and sailed.

21:3 We kept Cyprus on the boat's left
As the island met our eyes,
Then kept sailing to Syria,
Where the ship would unload supplies.

We landed at Tyre to unload.
21:4 So we sought out disciples there
And stayed with them for seven days.
Of our plan they were made aware.*

Through the Spirit they kept begging
For Paul to make up his mind
Not to go to Jerusalem,
But their begging he declined.*

21:5 Later we left to board the ship
When seven days did expire.
With wives and kids they walked with us
To the beach outside of Tyre.

After we knelt and prayed with them,
Farewells were exchanged with each.
21:6 We climbed on board the sailing ship,
And they went home from the beach.

21:7 Having finished the course from Tyre,
To Ptolemais we attained.
After greeting the brothers there,
One day with them we remained.

21:8 Leaving from there on the next day,
To Caesarea we reached.
We entered into Philip's house,
The evangelist who preached.

Philip was one of the seven.
We stayed with him in his home.
21:9 Philip had four virgin daughters.
As prophetesses they were known.

21:10 We had been staying in his home
For quite some days when there came
From Judea a prophet of God.
Agabus was the man's name.

21:11 Agabus took Paul's belt and said,
After coming over to us
And binding his own hands and feet,
"The Holy Spirit speaks thus:

"'The Jews within Jerusalem
Will likewise fulfill their plans,
Binding the man who owns this belt,
Giving him to Gentile hands.'"

21:12 Then as we heard all of these words,
Both we and the locals there,
Begged that up to Jerusalem
Paul not walk into that snare.

21:13 Paul responded, "What's this crying?
You are all breaking my heart.
I'm fully ready to be bound,
Even from life to depart.

"I'm ready for Jerusalem
To be bound, to even die
For the name of the Lord Jesus.
To dissuade me, do not try."*

21:14 When we realized he would not hear
Anything or anyone,
We kept silent, saying just this,
"The will of the Lord be done."

21:15 After those days, packing our things,
Up to Jerusalem we went.
21:16 Disciples from Caesarea
Came with us *on the ascent.

They brought us all to Mnason's home
Where we were to stay and rest.
He was an early disciple
From Cyprus, *to the northwest.

21:17 When we came to Jerusalem,
The brothers' welcome was pleasant.
21:18 Then next, Paul went with us to James,
And all the elders were present.

21:19 After giving salutations,
Paul explained, no detail shirked,
How the Lord among the Gentiles
Had through his ministry worked.

21:20 Hearing this, they were praising God,
And then spoke these words to Paul:
"Notice, brother, how many Jews
Are believers. *It's not small!

"There are thousands among the Jews.
For the Law they all have zeal.
21:21 They've been told that you've been teaching
Another kind of ideal.

"They think you're teaching all the Jews
Who among the Gentiles abide,
That as for the Laws of Moses,
They are not to be applied.

"'Stop circumcising your children!
Observe no customs at all!'
This is what they all are hearing
About the teaching of Paul.

21:22 "So therefore, how must we respond?
They've all heard that you've come now.
21:23 Do exactly what we tell you.
We've four men under a vow.

21:24 "With these four men make yourself clean,
And pay all their expenses
So that all their heads can be shaved,
And end the rumored offenses.

"For all the things against you said
The Jews will have to withdraw
Since they will see just how you live,
Keeping and guarding the Law.

21:25 "We told the Gentiles who believe
In written communication,
'Abstain from idol meats and blood,
Strangled foods and fornication.'"

21:26 The next day Paul took those four men
And with them made himself pure.
He went into the temple courts,
The sacrifices to secure.

The end of purification
Before the priests he conveyed
So at that time the sacrifice
For each of them would be made.

21:27 The seven days were almost up
To fulfill what Paul had vowed,
When Asian Jews at the temple
Saw him and stirred up the crowd.

Then with their hands they captured Paul,
21:28 Crying out to the multitude,
"Men of Israel, come to our aid.
This man's work must be subdued.*

"He teaches all in every place
Against us Jews and our law.
He teaches against the temple,
Having no respect, no awe.*

"Furthermore, into the temple
Greek people this man has brought,
And has defiled this holy place.
The troublemaker we've got!"*

21:29 (For Trophimus, the Ephesian,
With Paul in town they had viewed.
That Paul brought him to the temple
Is what they came to conclude.)

21:30 The whole city became stirred up,
Rushed together as one opposed.
Out of the temple they dragged Paul,
And at once the doors were closed.

21:31 As they were seeking to kill him,
The cohort's captain got word
That Jerusalem, all of it,
Had become violently stirred.

21:32 At once he took with him soldiers,
Their centurions as well,
And descended upon the crowd,
The violence to dispel.*

When the crowd saw all the soldiers
With their captain rushing in,
They stopped beating up on Paul.
21:33 Then the captain arrested him.

He ordered Paul to be restrained
By two chains instead of one.
He was asking who Paul might be
And what actions he had done.

21:34 Among the crowd came different shouts,
And since he could not detect
Any truth due to the uproar,
To leave he had to elect.

He ordered Paul to the barracks.
21:35 The crowd's force became so strong
As Paul happened upon the steps
That he could not move along.

The soldiers had to carry him,
21:36 But the crowd followed and cried,
"Away with him! Away with him!"
As long as Paul was outside.

21:37 Paul was just about to be led
Inside the base out of view
When he turned to ask the captain,
"May I say something to you?"

The captain said, "Do you know Greek?
21:38 The Egyptian you are not
Who stirred up a great rebellion
And led a seditious plot.

"You are not the person who led
Four thousand murderous men
In the desert some time ago.
So tell me, who are you then?"*

21:39 Paul said, "I am a citizen
From no ordinary place,
From Tarsus in Cilicia.
And I am a Jew by race.

"I'm begging you, please let me speak
To this people, to this crowd."
21:40 So the captain permitted him.
To speak to them he allowed.

Then Paul motioned to the people
As on the stairs he stood erect.
When the people quieted down,
He spoke in their dialect.

22:1 "You men, both brothers and fathers!"
In Hebrew to them he cried,
"Please listen now to my defense
Which I offer you outside."

22:2 When they heard that the Hebrew tongue
Was being spoken by Paul,
They quieted down even more
As he explained to them all.

22:3 "I myself am a Jewish man,
Not born on this city's earth.
In Tarsus of Cilicia
Was the city of my birth.

"Yet I was raised in this city
At the famed Gamaliel's feet
According to ancestral law,
The strictest standards to meet.

"I was zealous concerning God
As you are this very day,
22:4 Persecuting even to death
Those belonging to the Way.

"I'd arrest and deliver them
To prisons wherein to dwell.
I did not just do this to men
But to the women as well.

22:5 “Both the high priest and the elders
Can verify what I say,
For from them I received letters
To our brothers *against the Way.

“To Damascus I went to bring
Everyone who had been chained
Back here into Jerusalem,
Their sentence to be obtained.

22:6 “But while going to Damascus
As I was nearing the town,
Right in the middle of the day
The unexpected shined down.

“A great light flashed all around me.
From heaven this light did fall.
22:7 I fell right then onto the ground,
And I heard a voice say, ‘Saul!

“‘Saul, why do you persecute Me?’
22:8 ‘Who are You, sir?’ I replied;
‘I am Jesus of Nazareth,
Whom you pursue and deride.’

22:9 “Now all the men who were with me
Were able to see the light,
But they understood not the voice,
And they were all filled with fright.

22:10 “I said, ‘O sir! What should I do?’
He said, ‘Get up and proceed
Into Damascus. You’ll bc told
Your tasks that have been decreed.’

22:11 "But since I was completely blind
From the brightness of that light,
Into Damascus I was led
By those with me. They had sight.*

22:12 "There came a man, Ananias,
Devout as gauged by the Law,
Well-spoken of by all Jews there
Who his pious lifestyle saw.

22:13 "While standing next to me he said,
'Brother Saul, your sight receive!'
The moment that he said those words
Him I could clearly perceive.

22:14 "He said, 'The God of our fathers
Has chosen you, it is clear,
His will to know, the Just One to see,
The sound of His voice to hear.

22:15 "'You'll testify to all mankind
Of what you have seen and heard.
22:16 So what are you still waiting for?
Get up and obey His word.

"'Get yourself baptized, your sins cleansed
As you call upon His name;'
22:17 Sometime later after all this,
To Jerusalem I came.

"I was praying in the temple
When I fell into a trance.
22:18 I saw the Lord saying to me,
'To be heard you'll have no chance.

"'Quickly exit Jerusalem,
For those here will not receive
What you have to say about Me.
So do not delay, now leave!'

22:19 "But I said, 'Lord! They know me well,
That in every synagogue
All those who placed their faith in You
I did jail and flog.

22:20 "'When Stephen's blood was being shed,
I stood by with full consent,
Guarding the clothes of the stoners
As they killed your testament.'

22:21 "But then the Lord replied to me,
'You must now depart from here,
For I will send you far away
To the Gentiles, their frontier.'

22:22 Up until this final statement,
Their attention they did give.
"Rid such one from the earth," they yelled,
"For he is not fit to live!"

22:23 As they were shouting angrily,
Throwing down their outer clothes
And throwing dust into the air,
22:24 To step in, the captain chose.

He ordered Paul to the barracks.
Then said, "Beat the answers out.
Question him so that we can know
Why they rant and rave and shout."

22:25 Paul said to the centurion
Who was standing there nearby
As he was being tied with straps,
"To this question please reply.

"Is it lawful for you or not
To let a flogging extend
Unto a Roman citizen
Although he is not condemned?"

22:26 When the centurion heard this,
His captain he went to advise,
"Since he's a Roman citizen,
Whatever you do, be wise."*

22:27 The captain went to Paul and asked,
"Are you a Roman? Reply!"
Paul answered with a simple yes.
22:28 The captain spoke on to pry.*

"I obtained this citizenship
With money, a tidy sum."
Paul replied back, "Not so with me.
By birth this I have become."

22:29 The ones about to question him
Withdrew leaving Paul alone.
The captain then became afraid
For binding a man of Rome.

22:30 The captain planned to find the facts
Of the Jews' accusation.
So the next day he released Paul
And called a convocation.

The chief priests, the whole Sanhedrin,
To attend he gave command.
When they assembled, he brought Paul
And before them had him stand.

23:1 Then Paul addressed the Sanhedrin
As on them he fixed his gaze,
"Men, brothers, I've lived before God
In good conscience all my days."

23:2 But the high priest Ananias
Ordered those standing near Paul
To strike his mouth for speaking up,
For having the nerve, the gall.*

23:3 But Paul replied, "You whitewashed wall!
God will strike you by His hand.
You sit to judge me by the Law
But break it by this command."

23:4 Those standing next to Paul replied,
"The high priest of God you curse!"
23:5 Paul answered back, "I did not know,
For it's written in this verse:

"'Concerning your people's ruler,
Against him you must not speak.'
I knew him not as the high priest
Who said, 'Strike him on the cheek.'"

23:6 Now Paul knew that the Sanhedrin
Had within opposing views.[218]
Sadducees and Pharisees sat
On this council of the Jews.

"I'm a Pharisee and one's son,"
To the council Paul yelled and said.
"I am on trial for the hope
And resurrection from the dead!"

23:7 As soon as Paul yelled out these words,
Division it incited.
The Pharisees and Sadducees
No longer were united.

23:8 For Sadducees do not believe
That the dead will rise one day.
"There's no spirit; there's no angel."
Is what the Sadducees say.

The Pharisees, however, say
Spirits and angels exist,
And that the dead will rise again.
23:9 So division did persist.

Some scribal Pharisees rose up,
"No judgment do we invoke!
What if to him a spirit came,
Or an angel to him spoke?"

23:10 The captain feared as tension grew
That Paul's body they would shred.
He ordered soldiers to grab Paul
And into the barracks head.

23:11 Now the next night the Lord stood there
Next to Paul to make this known,
"You've declared Me in Jerusalem,
So also you must in Rome."

23:12 When morning came, the Jews conspired
And said, "Until we kill Paul,
We will not eat nor will we drink,
Or else may God curse us all."[219]

23:13 There were over forty of them
Involved in this plot to kill.
23:14 They told the chief priests and elders
Exactly what was their will.

"We've bound ourselves under a curse
That until we kill this Paul,
We will taste nothing, food nor drink,
Or else may God curse us all.

23:15 "Therefore, you and the Sanhedrin
Tell the captain, 'Bring Paul here!
So you can give a strict exam.'
We'll kill him before he comes near."

23:16 The son of the sister of Paul
Heard about this evil scheme.
He entered into the barracks,
Telling Paul of the unforeseen.

23:17 Paul summoned a centurion,
"To the captain take this youth.
He has inside information.
The captain must know the truth."

23:18 To the captain the youth was brought.
The soldier did not refuse.
"The prisoner Paul had me bring
This youth who has vital news."

23:19 The captain took him by the hand
And led him away from there,
Then inquired of him privately,
"What vital news do you bear?"

23:20 "The Jews agreed that tomorrow
They'd send you this supplication,
That you bring Paul to the council
For a strict examination.

23:21 "But do not be convinced by them,
For men more than forty strong
Are hidden as they wait for Paul,
Ready to commit a wrong.

"They've bound themselves under an oath
That until they murder Paul,
They will not eat, nor will they drink,
Else God's curse be on them all.

"The murderers are waiting now
At a secret location,
Expecting you to promise Paul
For the examination."

23:22 Then the captain let the youth go,
After giving this command:
"Tell no one that you informed me
Of anything, understand?"

23:23 Two centurions he then called,
"Go prepare to move along
Soldiers, spearmen, two hundred each,
And horsemen seventy strong.

"Then at the third hour of this night
To Caesarea you'll ride.
23:24 Bring Paul to Governor Felix
Safely on mounts you provide."

23:25 Then the captain wrote a letter
To send with this delegation.
What follows here is that letter,
That is, its replication:

23:26 "Sent from Claudius Lysias
To his highest excellence,
The ruling governor Felix.
May grace unto you dispense.

23:27 "This man was seized by Jewish men,
Almost robbed of life on earth,
But with my troops I rescued him,
For he is a Roman by birth.

23:28 "Determined to know the reason
For all their allegations,
I brought him to their Sanhedrin
For legal explanations.*

23:29 "I found that he was being charged
For matters about their law.
Not one charge was worthy of death
Or of prison that I saw.

23:30 "After I was told that a plot
Against this man was in place,
I sent him to you right away
For you to handle this case.

"For I ordered his accusers
To all come before your face
And explain to you everything
That has to do with this case."

23:31 Thus the soldiers did as ordered
By picking up Paul at night.
They brought him to Antipatris,
About a forty mile flight.[220]

23:32 On the next day the soldiers left,
Returning back to their base,
But the horsemen, they left with Paul,
Who continued with the pace.*

23:33 Arriving at Caesarea,
To the governor they went.
They handed over Paul to him
With the letter the captain sent.

23:34 Reading the letter, he asked Paul
Just what province he was from.
Learning it was Cilicia,
He told Paul what would be done.

23:35 "I will hear what you have to say
After your accusers come."
Then he ordered Paul to be kept
In Herod's Praetorium.

24:1 Five days later, the high priest came
With some elders of the Jews
And a lawyer named Tertullus
Who would represent their views.*

Ananias was the high priest
Who came with them for this case.
They brought their charges against Paul
Before the governor's face.

24:2 After Paul was called to appear,
Tertullus began to say,
"Because of you, noble Felix,
There's abundant peace each day.

"Because of you and your foresight,
This nation is greatly improved
24:3 In all places and in all ways.
With thankfulness we are moved.

24:4 "So as not to hinder your work,
A brief hearing I request
In the presence of your fairness
On the charges we have pressed.

24:5 "We've found this man as a nuisance.
Jews riot through his affect.
He travels throughout the Empire
And leads the Nazarene sect.

24:6 "He tried to profane the temple,
But we put him under arrest.[221]
24:8 As you yourself examine him,
You'll prove these charges we've pressed."

24:9 The Jewish men who came along
Joined in the verbal assault,
Claiming all that Tertullus said
Was precise and without fault.

24:10 The governor motioned for Paul
To answer the allegation.
So Paul began, "For many years
You've been a judge to this nation.

"Therefore, I will cheerfully give
My defense to you and to them.
24:11 'Twas not more than twelve days ago
Since I came to Jerusalem.

"I came in order to worship.
You can verify all these facts.
24:12 They found me not in the temple
In argumentative acts.

"They found me not stirring a crowd
In synagogues nor in town.
24:13 They cannot prove to you the things
Against me that they now sound.

24:14 "But this I do confess to you
That according to the Way,
I serve the God of our fathers.
Yet it's heresy they say.

"I believe all which is written
In the Prophets and the Law.
24:15 Just like they do, I hope in God,
Awaiting what prophets foresaw.*

"For both the just and the unjust
Will be raised to life again.
24:16 In this hope a blameless conscience
I keep before God and men.

24:17 "After my absence for some years,
I came with alms for my nation
And to present a sacrifice
For my purification.

24:18 "They found me in the temple courts
As ceremonially clean.
They did not find me with a crowd
Or in a riotous scene.

24:19 "But certain Asiatic Jews
Should be here before you today
To bring their charges against me
If they have something to say.

24:20 "Otherwise, let these men themselves
Explain what crime they had found
When before the Sanhedrin court
I testified with hands bound.[222]

24:21 "Only while standing among them,
This one message I yelled and said,
'For this I'm judged by you today,
The resurrection from the dead!'"

24:22 Felix knew more about the Way
And adjourned them from that place.
"When Captain Lysias comes down,
I will determine your case."

24:23 He ordered the centurion
To guard Paul and to permit
Any of his own friends to come
To serve him as they saw fit.

24:24 After some days, Felix returned,
With Drusilla, his Jewish wife.
He sent for Paul to hear him speak
Of faith in Christ Jesus, *that life.

24:25 Paul talked with him of righteousness,
Self-restraint and what's to come,
Specifically the judgment day.
Then Felix said, "Paul, you're done!"

For Felix became terrified.
He said, "You're dismissed for now.
I'll summon you another day
When more time I can allow."

24:26 At the same time he hoped that Paul
Would give him a tidy sum.
So he sent for him frequently,
Talking with him one on one.

24:27 Two years later Felix stepped down.
Then Porcius Festus reigned.
Felix wanted to please the Jews
So had left Paul bound and chained.

25:1 Three days after Festus arrived
In the province of Judea,
He went up to Jerusalem
From the town of Caesarea.

25:2 There the chief priests made known to him
All the charges against Paul.
The Jewish leaders were there too,
Urging Festus not to stall.

25:3 They asked that to Jerusalem
Paul be sent without delay,
For they had planned to ambush Paul
And to kill him on his way.

This favor that they asked of him,
25:4 He denied and said of Paul,
"He will stay at Caesarea
And won't be transferred at all.*

"For I will be returning there
To Caesarea not long.
25:5 Let key leaders go down with me
And state there what he's done wrong."

25:6 Festus delayed a little bit,
Eight or ten days at the most,
Before going to Caesarea,
A city along the coast.[223]

The next morning Festus appeared
And sat on his judgment throne.
He commanded that Paul be brought.
25:7 Then the charges were made known.

For after Paul had been brought out,
Around him the leaders stood,
Jewish ones from Jerusalem
Who accused him all they could.

All the charges that they laid out
Carried some serious weight,
But none of the accusations
Could these men substantiate.

25:8 Paul then said in his own defense,
"Not against the Jewish law,
Or the temple, or the Caesar,
Have I sinned; I'm without flaw."

25:9 Festus said in reply to Paul,
Desiring to please the Jews,
"I'll try you in Jerusalem,
If this you're willing to choose."

25:10 Paul then replied, "I'm standing here
Before Caesar's judgment seat,
Which is where I ought to be tried.
In no other court will I meet.*

"For you yourself know very well
That I have not wronged the Jews,
25:11 But if I am a criminal,
Caesar's court you can't refuse.

"If I've done a capital crime,
I will not refuse to die.
None can grant this favor to them.
Their charges you must deny.

"There is only one choice to make.
My own rights no one can steal.
I am a Roman citizen
So to Caesar I appeal."[224]

25:12 Festus conferred with his council
As to what words to bestow,
Then said, "You've appealed to Caesar.
Then to Caesar you will go!"

25:13 Now King Agrippa and Bernice,
After some days had expired,
Traveled down to Caesarea,
Greeting Festus as newly hired.

25:14 Since they were staying many days,
Festus with the king conferred
About the case concerning Paul,
Reviewing all that was heard.

"There is this man left by Felix
As a prisoner," Festus said.
25:15 "When I went to Jerusalem,
Some Jews came to me and pled.

"The chief priests and elders these were
Who gave their accusation
That this man was worthy of death.
They begged his condemnation.

25:16 "I told them of the Roman law
That we can't give up a man
Before facing his accusers
To answer the best he can.

25:17 "Therefore, when they had gathered here,
I did not at all delay.
I sat upon the judgment seat
Early the very next day.

"I had the man brought to his foes
25:18 Who all stood up projecting
All the details against this man,
None which I was expecting.

25:19 "Over their own superstition
Their disagreements did thrive,
And over Jesus who is dead
But whom Paul said was alive.

25:20 "Not knowing how to work this out,
I asked if he wished to plot
A transfer to Jerusalem
To be tried on this or not.

25:21 "Paul then appealed to be detained
For the emperor's decision.
So until he goes to Caesar,
I've ordered him to prison."

25:22 Then Agrippa said to Festus,
"This man I might wish to hear."
Festus replied, "You will indeed!
Tomorrow Paul will appear."

25:23 On the next day Agrippa came
With Bernice in pompous décor.
With the captains and town leaders
They entered the hearing floor.

After Festus gave the command,
Paul was brought into that place.
25:24 "King Agrippa and all those here,"
He said pointing to Paul's face.[225]

"Notice the man standing right there.
All residents who are Jews,
Both here and in Jerusalem,
Tell me that he is bad news.

"They have cried out the same desire
That he must no longer live,
25:25 But when I learned the things he did,
That sentence I could not give.

"He's done nothing worthy of death,
But since he made his appeal
To be heard by the emperor,
I had to grant him that deal.

25:26 "But what to write unto my lord
I have not one factual thing.
So I brought Paul before you all
And you, Agrippa, O King!

"I hope I have something to write
From this hearing I've preferred.
25:27 For to send a captive uncharged
Seems to me to be absurd."

26:1 Then Agrippa declared to Paul,
"To speak you may now commence."
With hand motions Paul then began
To clarify his defense.

26:2 "With all the charges by the Jews,
I consider myself as blessed
To face you now, King Agrippa,
To answer the charges pressed.

26:3 "Since all of the Jewish customs
And disputes you know quite well,
Therefore, I beg that patiently
You listen to what I tell.

26:4 "My way of life from my youth up,
Which was spent among my own,
In the city, Jerusalem,
By all Jews is quite well known.

26:5 “They knew that from the beginning,
And if they wish to agree,
According to our strictest sect
I lived as a Pharisee.

26:6 “I am right now standing trial
For the promised hope God made
To our fathers of ancient time
26:7 On which our twelve tribes are stayed.

“For they serve God both night and day
As to this promise they cling.
About this hope I stand accused
By my fellow Jews, O King.

26:8 “Why do you deem impossible
That God resurrects the dead?”
Paul posed this question to the crowd,
And then to the king he said:[226]

26:9 “Now I myself thought it a must
To make a hostile campaign
Against all things connected with
Jesus of Nazareth’s name.

26:10 “I did this in Jerusalem,
But no law did I abuse,*
For I received authority
From the chief priests of the Jews.

“Not only did I jail the saints,
Against them I cast my stone.[227]
As they were being put to death,
All their deaths I did condone.

26:11 "The many times I punished them,
Them I would try to compel
In all the synagogues around
To speak blasphemy as well.

"But they did not speak blasphemy,*
Which made my anger expand.
So I chased them even as far
As the towns outside their land.

26:12 "One such chase was to Damascus
On the power and commission
By the chief priests of the Jews.
26:13 There I met my opposition.

"About midday while on the road,
I saw a heavenly light
Shining around me and my troops,
And it was extremely bright!

"'Twas brighter than the sun, O King.
26:14 So to the ground we all fell.
I heard a voice then speak to me
In Hebrew, which I know well.

"'O Saul, Saul, why persecute Me?
Why in this do you persist?
For you it is too difficult
To kick against prods and resist.'

26:15 "And so I asked, 'Who are You, sir?'
He said, 'He whom you mistreat.
I'm the One whom you persecute,
26:16 But rise and stand on your feet.

"'I have appeared to you for this
To make you My appointee,
Servant and witness to all you saw
And all you have yet to see.

26:17 "'I'll deliver you from the Jews
And from the Gentiles as well,
For I am sending you to them
For the reason I now tell:*

26:18 "'To open up their blinded eyes,
To turn them from darkness to light,
From Satan's power unto God,
That their sins be sent from God's sight.

"'Also that the inheritance
Among all the sanctified,
Those set apart by faith in Me,
Would to their account be applied.'

26:19 "Consequently, King Agrippa,
To this heavenly vision
I was not disobedient.
I had no indecision.

26:20 "But first to those in Damascus,
Then to Jerusalem I went,
Then throughout all of Judea
I preached that Jews should repent.

"To the Gentiles I preached the same,
To change and turn to the Lord,
And that all the deeds they practice
With repentance must accord.

26:21 “It is because of all these things
That the Jews did what they did,
Seizing me in the temple courts,
And my death to not forbid.

26:22 “Therefore, having received God’s help,
I’m standing this very day,
Witnessing to both small and great
Of what the prophets did say.

“For the prophets and Moses spoke
Of things yet centuries ahead,
26:23 Namely that the Christ would suffer
And rise again from the dead.

“This first signaled what Christ would do
To make His proclamations
Of light to the Jewish people
And to the Gentile nations.”

26:24 While Paul was making this defense,
With a loud voice Festus yelled,
“You’re crazy, Paul, from much learning.
To madness you’ve been propelled!”

26:25 Paul said, “Festus, most noble sir,
I’m not insane; there’s no doubt,
But words of truth and sound reason
From my own mouth just pour out.

26:26 “For the king knows about these things,
Before whom I boldly reply,
Since in a corner they weren’t done.
From his ears they did not slip by.

26:27 “King Agrippa, do you believe
The prophets who have foretold?
I know for sure that you believe
The inspired prophets of old.”*

26:28 Then Agrippa replied to him,
“In this space of time that’s small,
Do you think that your arguments
Will make me a Christian, Paul?”

26:29 “Little or much, I wish to God
That those hearing me today,
Also you, would become like me
Except for these chains, I say.”

26:30 After Paul’s words, the king arose,
The governor, and Bernice,
And all of those sitting with them,
26:31 But the meeting did not cease.*

They went aside and talked some more.
To one another they exclaimed,
“This man does nothing that deserves
For him to be jailed or chained!”

26:32 But Agrippa said to Festus,
“This man could have been set free
If an appeal to the Caesar
Would never have been his plea.”

27:1 When orders came for us to sail
To Italy for this case,
Paul, with some other prisoners,
Were brought to a shipping place.*

They were given to Julius
Of the Imperial band,
Leader of one hundred soldiers.[228]
They were given into his hand.

27:2 A ship from Adramyttium
Was about to leave the yard
To sail to the Asian coastlines.
So we boarded under guard.

Now a man named Aristarchus
Boarded with our committee.
He was from Macedonia,
A Thessalonian city.

27:3 The next day we docked at Sidon,
And being friendly and fair,
Julius let Paul meet his friends
So that for him they could care.

27:4 From there we sailed next to Cyprus,
Seeking the land's protection,
For the winds were unfavorable,
Against our ship's direction.

27:5 Cilicia, Pamphylia,
We sailed past, crossing the sea.
When we arrived at Lycia,
At Myra we stayed briefly.

27:6 There the commander Julius,
The centurion, had found
A ship from Alexandria
Which to Italy was bound.

He put us all on board that ship,
27:7 But we sailed with little gain
For a number of many days,
Reaching Cnidus with much strain.

Since the wind did not allow us
To go a straight direction,
We sailed around the isle of Crete
By Salmone for protection.

27:8 Even though it was difficult,
To a certain town we came
Near the city of Lasea.
Fair Havens was the town's name.

27:9 By then sailing was dangerous.
Much time had wasted away,
For then the Jewish fast had passed.
So Paul advised them to stay.

27:10 With insistence he said to them,
"This voyage, men, I perceive
Will meet with damage to the ship,
And great loss to us will cleave.

"Not just cargo will we all lose.
Many lives will also fall."
27:11 But the ship's piloting captain
Was more persuasive than Paul.

The centurion decided
That progress they should pursue,
Listening more to the captain
Than to Paul on what to do.

27:12 Since the harbor for wintering
Was unfit for any ship,
The majority determined
To continue with the trip.

They planned to winter in Phoenix,
A harbor which was in Crete,
Much better sheltered by the winds[229]
With which they could not compete.

27:13 When a south wind gently came up,
Thinking their plans would succeed,
They weighed anchor, and close to Crete
They just sailed along with speed.

27:14 Not very long into this trip,
A wind of tremendous force,
Better known as a Northeaster,
Blew from Crete onto our course.

27:15 Because the ship was caught off guard,
And the wind it could not face,
We gave way to the violent wind
And were driven at its pace.

27:16 The small island known as Cauda
Blocked us little from the storm.
The task of hoisting the lifeboat,
We just barely could perform.

27:17 Once hoisted up, cables they ran
To hold the ship together,
But they feared the Syrtis sandbars
In this turbulent weather.

So they lowered the sailing gear[230]
And were driven in this way.
27:18 Since we were being tossed about,
They threw cargo off the next day.

27:19 On the third day with their own hands,
They tossed the ship's sailing gear,
27:20 But for quite a number of days
No sun or stars did appear.

Because no sun or stars were seen
And the storm raged unimproved,
All hope for lives of being saved
Was abandoned, *was removed.

27:21 When they had not eaten for days,
Paul stood before all and said,
"You should not have set sail from Crete
But listened to me instead.

"All the damage upon this ship
And all loss would have been spared,
27:22 But now I urge, keep your courage.
There is no need to be scared.*

"For there will be no loss of life,
But damage will be widespread.
27:23 An angel of the God I serve
Stood by me last night and said:

27:24 "'O Paul, now stop being afraid.
Before Caesar you must stand.
God has granted safety to all,
Giving them into your hand.'

27:25 "Therefore, O men, keep your courage,
For to faith in God I hold.
I believe that it will happen
Precisely as I've been told.

27:26 "But we will have to run aground
On a certain island ahead.
As to which island this will be,*
In the message it was not said."*

27:27 Across the Adriatic sea
The storm was driving our ship.
At midnight the sailors sensed land,
The fourteenth night of our trip.

27:28 They took soundings to check the depth
Of the water that was below.
It was one hundred twenty feet,
But shrinking while on the go.*

For soon after they checked again,
It was ninety feet that turn.
27:29 Fearing we would be dashed on rocks,
They dropped anchors from the stern.

Four anchors the sailors lowered,
Yearning for daylight to come.
27:30 They went and lowered the lifeboat.
Under pretense this was done.

They pretended that the anchors
Needed lowering from the bow.
27:31 As these men were about to leave,
Paul saw them and would not allow.

For Paul to the centurion
And to the soldiers declared,
"If those men don't stay on this ship,
Your own lives will not be spared."

27:32 The soldiers acted right away,
Cutting the ropes of the boat
That were joining it to the ship,
And they let it freely float.

27:33 Right up until the daylight came,
Paul implored with common sense,
"You've gone without food fourteen days
While anxiously in suspense.

27:34 "Therefore, I urge that you all eat.
You need not worry at all.*
Take nourishment for your own health.
No hair from your head will fall."

27:35 Having said this, Paul took some bread,
Thanking God in public view,
And broke a piece off for himself.
The food he began to chew.

27:36 Encouraged by the words of Paul,
They ate for their health to fix.
27:37 The number of those on the ship
Was two hundred seventy-six.

27:38 When they all had eaten their fill,
They took the grain that was stored
And began to lighten the load
By throwing it overboard.

27:39 When daylight came, they saw some land,
Not familiar to anyone.
They spotted a bay with a beach
Onto which they planned to run.

27:40 They cut the ropes to the anchors
Which sank to the ocean floor,
Loosed the helm's ropes, raised the mainsail,
And let the wind drive them to shore.

27:41 But the ship struck a sandbar fast.
The bow could not move at all
While the stern was dashed to pieces
By waves coming from the squall.

27:42 The soldiers came up with a plan.
The prisoners they would slay
In order that no prisoner
Would flee by swimming away.

27:43 But because the centurion
Had Paul's safety already planned,
He kept their scheme from happening
By giving his own command.

He commanded all the able
To first jump out of the boat
And swim directly to the land.
27:44 The rest were to go afloat.

Any plank or thing from the boat
They grabbed and held by each hand.
All two hundred seventy-six
Were brought safely to the land.

28:1 After safely reaching the land,
We found out the island's name.
It was the island of Malta.
28:2 With kindness the natives[231] came.

Although they were barbarians,
No kindness did they withhold.
They took us in and made a fire
Because of the rain and cold.

28:3 When Paul brought sticks and added them,
The temperature to expand,
Out of the heat a viper came
And locked its fangs on his hand.

28:4 The natives said, watching it hang,
"A killer this man must be.
His punishment of death this is
Although he escaped the sea."

28:5 Paul shook the snake into the fire.
All ill effects from him fled.
The natives thought he would swell up
Or would swiftly fall down dead.

28:6 After watching him for some time
And seeing no harm occur,
They changed their minds and then proclaimed
That he was a god for sure.

28:7 A certain man named Publius,
Who owned many lands nearby,
Who also was the island's chief,
Welcomed us in great supply.

For three full days he boarded us.
His kindness was unwary.
28:8 While we were there, his father fell sick
To fevers and dysentery.

Paul came into the sick man's room,
And right after he had prayed,
Healed the man of all his sickness
While on him his hands he laid.

28:9 Now after this everyone else
From the island came to Paul,
That is, all those plagued with disease.
He brought healing to them all.

28:10 They honored us with great honors.
Many gifts on us they poured.
When we sailed they supplied our needs,
Loading the supplies on board.

28:11 Now wintering on the island
Was an Alexandrian ship,
Painted with the twin sons of Zeus.
On it we resumed our trip.

After three months on the island,
28:12 Up to Syracuse we sailed.
We remained there for three more days.
28:13 Then to Rhegium we trailed.[232]

We had to tack to reach this port,
But the next day a south wind blew,
Which brought us to Puteoli,
Not on that day but day two.

28:14 There we found some of the brothers,
Believers, *that is to say.
For one week we were invited
By these believers to stay.

And in that way we came toward Rome,
28:15 For the Roman brothers heard
That we were on our way to Rome.
So to meet us they were stirred.

At the Forum of Appius,
About forty miles from Rome,*
The first group intercepted us.
Their encouragement was shown.

At the city called Three Taverns,
About thirty miles from Rome,*
The next group intercepted us.
Their encouragement was shown.

At the mere sight of these brothers,
To God Paul gave gratitude.
For by coming all of that way,
It greatly improved his mood.

28:16 When we reached the city of Rome,
Paul was permitted, not barred,
To stay in a house by himself
With a soldier there to guard.

28:17 Three days later, Paul then summoned
The chief leaders of the Jews.
When they all had come together,
Paul proclaimed to them this news:

"O men, brothers, although I've done
Nothing wrong against our race
Or against our fathers' customs,
I'm a prisoner before your face.

"I was jailed in Jerusalem,
Then put into Roman hands.
28:18 After they had examined me,
To release me was their plans.

"For not one thing worthy of death
In my deeds could one reveal,
28:19 But when the Jews protested this,
I was compelled to appeal.

"I appealed to Caesar of Rome
So that he should hear my case,
Not that I held one single thing
Against my own Hebrew race.

28:20 "Because of this, I requested
To meet with you and explain,
For it's because of Israel's hope
That I am bound with this chain."

28:21 They answered him, "From Judea
We've no letters on you, Paul,
Nor have any brothers declared
Any evil on you at all.

28:22 "But we do want to hear your views,
For every one of us knows
That everywhere against your sect
The opposition just grows."

28:23 So they arranged a certain day
To hear all his points of view.
They came to his place of lodging
With many more than a few.

Testifying of God's kingdom,
Paul explained from dawn 'til dark,
Attempting to persuade them all
With each scriptural remark.*

He went through the Law of Moses
And all the Prophets as well,
Pointing out to them the Scriptures
Which of Jesus did foretell.

28:24 Some were convinced by what Paul said.
Some believed not what they heard.
28:25 Since they could not agree, they left,
But not before Paul's last word.

"To your fathers the Spirit spoke
Through the prophet's words so right
28:26 When he told Isaiah to go
And tell the people their plight.

"'You will go on your way and hear,
But knowledge to you won't cleave.
You will go on your way and see,
But you will never perceive.

28:27 "'For this people's hearts became hard
And their ears can scarcely hear.
Even their eyes have become closed,
Otherwise, Me they would fear.*

"'If with their eyes they truly saw,
And if with their ears they heard,
If with their hearts they understood,
To heal them I would be stirred.'

28:28 "Therefore, let it be known to you
That this salvation of God
Has been sent to those who will hear,
The Gentiles, here and abroad."[233]

28:30 For two full years in his own house,
At his own expense, Paul stayed.
He also welcomed everyone
Who to him a visit paid.

28:31 He kept preaching of God's kingdom
And teaching with bold intent
All about the Lord Jesus Christ,
And this no one did prevent.

ENDNOTES

1 Implied.
2 Poetic elaboration on this Jewish custom outlined in the Mishnah (Tamid 5:2). A priest could only receive this privilege once in his lifetime.
3 Derived from Numbers 6:3.
4 Literally, *after those days.*
5 Literally, *behold*, which is a call to pay close attention.
6 Implied. This prophecy may be the praises referred to in verse 64.
7 Not stated by Luke. The oath is found in Genesis 22:16–18.
8 Literally, *you will be called.*
9 Literally, *that which is inhabited*, referring to the population of the Roman Empire.
10 The word *Christ* means *Anointed One.*
11 Poetic elaboration on the word *peace*. Peace between God and man is due to Jesus's work on the cross (Romans 5:1).
12 Literally, *just as was spoken to them.*
13 Poetic elaboration. This custom was observed in the naming of John the Baptist as recorded in Luke 1:59–63.
14 Derived from Leviticus 12:7, 8.
15 Literally, *to the Lord.*
16 Derived from Leviticus 12:7, 8.
17 Poetic elaboration on the meaning of *Christ.*
18 Derived from Exodus 1:4 and Revelation 7:4–8.
19 Poetic elaboration. There is disagreement as to whether Hannah was eighty-four years old at this time or if Luke did not know her age but only that she was married for seven years and widowed for eighty-four years. If the latter, she would be at least 104 years old. This would be certainly worth noting.
20 Literally, *the Law of the Lord.*
21 This information is derived from Leviticus 23:4–8.
22 *of the Law* is not used by Luke to describe the teachers.
23 Literally, *Behold.*

24 Some translators think this to be an idiom meaning, *in My Father's house*, referring to Genesis 41:51. But Genesis refers not to a place (house) but people (household). The Greek here literally reads, *in the things of My Father*.

25 Literally, *was written in the book*.

26 Derived from Mark 6:17.

27 Not stated by Luke. The voice quotes Psalm 2:7, *This is My Son, My beloved*, and Isaiah 42:1, *In You I obtain delight*.

28 The genealogy here differs from the genealogy of Joseph's line in Matthew 1. Luke emphasizes that Joseph was assumed to be Jesus's father but implies the assumption to be wrong. So he goes to the first male in Jesus's line, which would be Mary's father, Eli. Luke is tracing Jesus's physical ancestry, which goes through Mary, not Joseph.

29 The Greek text reads, *of Eli, of Matthat ... of God*. The word *son* is implied. The word *son* is used loosely to refer to physical ancestry. So Jesus was Eli's son in the sense of being his grandson. This pattern continues through Adam. But then the pattern is broken in referring to God. God brought about Jesus's human existence miraculously without the aid of a human father. Therefore, Jesus is the Son of God. See Luke 1:34, 35. Much poetic license is used in this genealogy to create rhyme.

30 Ezra 2:2.

31 The Greek text is the exact same spelling as Jesus; many translations revert to the Hebrew equivalent of Joshua.

32 See 1 Chronicles 3:5.

33 1 Samuel 17:14, 15

34 Ruth 4:13.

35 *Salmon* is Hebrew; *Sala* is the Greek spelling that Luke reports.

36 Genesis 6:13, 14.

37 Genesis 5:27.

38 Genesis 5:24.

39 Luke spells this name in the Greek the same as verse 36; but many versions spell it differently to correspond with the Hebrew in Genesis 5:12.

40 See Genesis 4:26.

41 Literally, *He hungered*.

42 Derived from Matthew 4:8. Luke records that Satan led Jesus up but does not specify anything further.

43 Literally, *it has been said*. Deuteronomy 6:16 is a message from the Lord communicated by Moses.

44 Derived from Mark 1:22–27.

45 Luke does not say that Jesus was appointed. This was the Jewish custom of the Haphtarah, where a person was appointed to read from the prophets and then to comment on the reading.

46 Implied.

47 Literally, *Physician, heal yourself.*
48 Derived from Mark 1:22.
49 This is no doubt the same Simon whose house Jesus visited back in 4:38, Simon Peter.
50 Derived from Mark 3:17.
51 Implied.
52 Jesus was not forbidding the man to never tell of his healing but to follow the Law in Leviticus 14 as testimony of his cleansing. This would take a week. Mark 1:45 indicates that the man disobeyed, immediately telling people of his healing, which caused too great of crowds.
53 Literally, *to place before Him*, referring to Jesus.
54 Derived from verse 26.
55 Literally, *and he was following Him.*
56 The guests are actively celebrating with joy in the presence of the bridegroom.
57 Derived from Luke 5:10.
58 Derived from Matthew 5:4.
59 Literally, *sons of the Highest One.*
60 The last two lines are derived from the centurion's message.
61 Literally, *to the Lord.*
62 Literally, *John the Baptist.*
63 Literally, *John's messengers.*
64 Implied.
65 Implied.
66 Jesus refers to three customary actions toward an honored guest—washing the feet with water, greeting the guest with a kiss, and anointing the head with oil.
67 *what's hidden from view* is the meaning of *mysteries.*
68 Jesus is combining the two parables, showing the correlation of what is true in those who hear and what will be revealed about them.
69 Implied.
70 Literally, *saw what had happened.*
71 Literally, *what had happened.*
72 Derived from Malachi 4:5.
73 Derived from John 6:12.
74 Poetic elaboration on the word Christ.
75 Derived from Mark 8:34.
76 Literally, *Son of Man.*
77 Implied from the Greek text. *You* is in the plural in the Greek text when referring to the people of that generation. But the command to bring the son is in the singular.
78 Derived from Mark 9:20.
79 Literally, *Jesus, knowing.*
80 Implied.

81 The words in brackets are not found in the best manuscripts.
82 Derived from the next verse.
83 The lawyer did not want to say, *The Samaritan*, because of the hatred he had toward them.
84 The last two lines are poetic elaboration. It was common knowledge that rabbis taught their followers what topics to cover in prayer.
85 The action words are in the Greek present tense, which emphasizes ongoing action. The parable was about persistence, and so one must not ask, seek, and knock only one time but with persistence.
86 The series of questions by Jesus are rhetorical questions expecting the answer no, which is clear in the Greek text.
87 Literally, *by Beelzebul.*
88 This is a rhetorical question expecting the answer yes.
89 This information, though not stated by Luke, was known to those who were familiar with the arrangement of the synagogues.
90 See Numbers 19:16.
91 The lawyers, commonly called scribes, belonged to either the sect of the Pharisees or the Sadducees.
92 No doubt Jesus was referring to the traditional man-made rules.
93 Literally, *will be proclaimed upon the rooftops.*
94 Implied.
95 Implied.
96 The three lines previous and two lines following are not repeated by Jesus.
97 Derived from the next verse.
98 Literally, *three sata*, which equals about one bushel or sixty pounds of whole wheat.
99 The content of His teaching is not stated, but He certainly included this as implied by the question raised in the next verse.
100 The implication is that they were watching to see if He would violate one of their Sabbath laws.
101 Poetic elaboration on the word *dropsy*, which derives from the Greek word for *water*. Fluid built up in this man's body, producing a bloated appearance.
102 Derived from verse 10.
103 Derived from the next verses and Philippians 3:8.
104 Derived from verse 27.
105 It is implied from the story that the sons were full grown.
106 The Greek word for *pod* means *little horn*, which was the shape of the pods on the carob tree common in the land of Israel.
107 More literally, *to celebrate and rejoice.*
108 A liquid measure of about 8.1 gallons.
109 A dry measure of about 10 bushels.

110 Literally, *they are barging in*. The picture here is of the enormous positive response to the preaching of God's kingdom. The Pharisees criticized the very response to which the Law and the Prophets looked forward.

111 From Exodus 20:14.

112 The penalty given in Exodus 20:14.

113 Implied.

114 Implied.

115 Two mulberry trees existed in this area, white and black. The black mulberry tree is the sycamore, and the white is the sycamine. Luke distinguishes between the two. See 19:4 for the sycamore.

116 *You* is more accurately *he*.

117 Literally, *what is commanded*. The contextual implication is to go beyond what is commanded in the Law—to encourage your brother to repent, to forgive your brother over and over again, to have a growing faith. Faith as a mustard seed.

118 Derived from Deuteronomy 24:8 and Leviticus 13–14.

119 Most versions translate as *made you well*, but it literally means *saved*. The context determines from what the person is saved. If the faith of the Samaritan saved him from leprosy, what healed the other nine lepers? The implication is that the Samaritan responded to his healing with faith, and the others did not. His faith saved him.

120 Derived from verse 30.

121 Literally, *in that day*.

122 Verse 36, though genuine in Matthew 24:40, was not recorded by Luke. He already included the words in verse 31.

123 They went to pray in an area of the temple where the general public gathered.

124 More literally, *they will never enter it*.

125 Literally, *The kingdom of God*.

126 Being a chief tax collector, Zacchaeus probably had other tax collectors serving under him.

127 Literally, *sycamore*. See 17:6 notes.

128 It is implied that the master said the same thing to this slave.

129 Implied.

130 Derived from verse 28.

131 More literally, *of visitation*.

132 Jesus is referring to Isaiah 56:7.

133 Implied.

134 Literally, *take the wife*, which is a reference to marriage.

135 Literally, *marry and are given in marriage*, covering both the male and the female.

136 Literally, *neither marry nor are given in marriage*.

137 Implied.

138 Poetic elaboration. In 20 BC, King Herod began remodeling the temple. See John 2:20.
139 Poetic elaboration. The application of the parable is twofold. First, verse 31 is the application to the signs of Christ's coming, which He explained in verses 25–28. Second, verses 32–36 is the application to the signs of the destruction of the temple that took place forty years later, which He explained in verses 20–24.
140 Literally, *rise early*.
141 Verses 43 and 44 are absent in many early Greek manuscripts. Some suggest that it was a historical event preserved through oral tradition that some copyists tried to work into Matthew and Luke.
142 Derived from John 18:19.
143 Implied.
144 Verse 17 is omitted by the earliest manuscripts and is found in some manuscripts after verse 19 in various forms. Its insertion was to explain the crowd's reaction as Matthew 27:15 and Mark 15:6 do.
145 Literally, *Jesus*.
146 Literally, *blessed are the barren*.
147 Derived from John 19:23, 24.
148 Literally, *until the ninth hour*, which according to the Jewish method of time was three o'clock in the afternoon.
149 Derived from Mark 15:34.
150 Derived from the following verses of burial procedures out of respect for the dead.
151 Implied.
152 Literally, *Lord Jesus*.
153 Derived from verse 20.
154 *To be broken* is derived from their attitude in verse 17.
155 Implied.
156 More literally, *the Law of Moses*.
157 Luke just lists their names. Poetic elaboration abounds in this list.
158 Literally, *the Holy Spirit*.
159 This is not in the Greek, although many versions insert it to clarify to the reader that Luke is picking up from Peter's words in verse 17 after inserting his own comments in verses 18 and 19.
160 Poetic elaboration. Peter quotes Psalm 69:25 first and then Psalm 109:8.
161 *without bias* is poetic elaboration.
162 Implied.
163 Poetic elaboration. See 2 Peter 1:20, 21.
164 Psalm 110:1 quote. The Hebrew has *Yahweh* for the first occurrence of the word *Lord*, which most Old Testament translators put in all capital letters. The second occurrence of the word *Lord* is the Hebrew word *adonai*, which translators did not put in all capital letters. This word commonly means *master*.

165 Literally, *you will receive.*
166 *in the name of Christ* is derived from Acts 2:38.
167 Derived from verse 24.
168 Poetic elaboration. Luke assumes that the reader knows about the Jewish law that did not permit trials at night. They had regard for that law in the case of Peter and John, but not so in the case of Jesus.
169 See Psalm 2:2. *His Son* is derived from Psalm 2:7.
170 *façade* is more literally *deed* and is derived from the implication of lying to God. The sin was not failing to give all of the proceeds but pretending to give it all.
171 More literally, *full of the Holy Spirit.*
172 *of disgrace* is poetic elaboration. To be called a Nazarene was contemptible. See John 1:46 and Matthew 2:23.
173 Derived from Genesis 42:7.
174 The promised time was four hundred years (Genesis 15:13).
175 Derived from Exodus 3:3.
176 Derived from Exodus 3:5
177 Literally, *The Holy Spirit.*
178 This sentence belongs to verse 16.
179 Verse 37 is not in the earliest Greek manuscripts.
180 Implied. The language indicates a miraculous transport of Philip by the Spirit to this city.
181 Derived from Acts 21:8.
182 Derived from verse 2.
183 Luke uses a favorite Greek phrase *egeneto de*, which is often translated by the KJV, *And it came to pass*. This phrase is found thirty-seven times in the New Testament and only in Luke and Acts. This phrase alerts the reader that time has passed. Sometimes Luke gives the amount of time that has passed (see Luke 6:1; 9:28; Acts 4:5; 5:7; 28:17); Many times he gives no time frame (see Luke 1:8; 5:1; Acts 16:16; 28:8). Only from Paul's own testimony in Galatians 1:13–19 do we know that this passage of time was three years.
184 Peter is referring to the dietary laws from the Old Covenant recorded in Leviticus 11.
185 Derived from 10:16.
186 Derived from 10:9.
187 Derived from 10:5.
188 Literally, *In the beginning*, but referring to the coming of the indwelling Holy Spirit to the Jewish believers (see John 14:17 and Acts 1:5, 8).
189 Literally, *the Lord Jesus Christ.*
190 Implied.
191 Literally *the Holy Spirit.*
192 Implied. The name was given to them by those outside the church.

193 More literally, *inhabited land* instead of *Rome's domain*. The same Greek word is found in Luke 2:1, which obviously means the Roman world, not the entire globe.
194 *in the dark* is implied from the context.
195 In the list of names that follows, information is taken from elsewhere to produce rhyme.
196 Acts 4:36.
197 Derived from verse 10.
198 Literally, *the Law of Moses*.
199 Literally, *the faith*.
200 Implied.
201 Implied.
202 Verse 34 is absent in the earliest Greek copies. This verse states that Silas stayed too. It was probably added to account for his presence in verse 40.
203 Derived from verse 3.
204 Literally, *having believed in God*.
205 Poetic elaboration. It was called the Egnatian Way.
206 Derived from verse 2.
207 More literally, *each one of us*.
208 Implied.
209 Implied.
210 Implied in the terminology employed by Luke.
211 It was about a seven-hundred-mile boat ride.
212 Literally, *the church*. Although Luke does not state it, the church was the Jerusalem church. Note the language throughout the Bible of people *going up* to Jerusalem regardless of direction. This was because of its elevation and its importance as the capital city.
213 Derived from 18:27, 28.
214 Implied.
215 Poetic elaboration here and within the list of names.
216 Implied.
217 Derived from verse 25.
218 Derived from verse 8.
219 The biblical text states that they bound themselves under a curse and does not quote their words here.
220 Antipatris was about forty miles north of Jerusalem.
221 Many later Greek manuscripts have more detail, the earliest being an eighth-century manuscript. Thus, some translations include this detail at the end of verse 6, verse 7, and the beginning of verse 8. All earlier Greek manuscripts do not contain this detail.
222 Derived from Acts 21:33. Paul was no doubt still bound when he stood before the Sanhedrin.
223 Caesarea was a port city located about sixty-five miles northwest of Jerusalem.

224 The first three lines of this stanza are poetic elaboration. Paul asserted his rights as a Roman citizen by appealing his case to Caesar to avoid any injustice by the hands of the Jews.

225 Implied in the next words.

226 The last two lines of this stanza are poetic elaboration. Paul is not addressing the king as he was in verse 7, since he uses the plural form of you in verse 8.

227 Literally, *a pebble*. A black pebble was a vote of guilty and a white pebble was a vote of not guilty.

228 Literally, *a centurion*, which was a commander of one hundred soldiers.

229 Luke's words may mean that the harbor faced the southwesterly and northwesterly winds or faced the same direction as these winds blew, northeast and southeast.

230 Literally, *lowering the vessel*. There is disagreement over whether the sails were lowered or the anchor.

231 The Greek is literally barbarians, a term used to describe those who could not speak Greek. They were called barbarians because Greeks would imitate foreign tribal tongues by saying, *Bar-bar*, several times. Later the term was used in a derogatory sense against foreigners, classifying them as uncivilized. Perhaps Luke uses this term to show that not all foreigners are uncivilized.

232 *trailed* is poetic elaboration based on the description of how they reached Rhegium. The Greek word has been used twice previously of *abandoning* hope (27:20) and *cutting loose* the anchors (27:40). It is translated as *remove* or *take away* in 2 Corinthians 3:16 and Hebrews 10:11. Therefore, they could not reach Rhegium on a direct route.

233 Verse 29 is not found in any Greek manuscript prior to the ninth century. Verse 25 has already stated how the Jews left.

www.ingramcontent.com/pod-product-compliance
Lightning Source LLC
Chambersburg PA
CBHW021051080526
44587CB00010B/205
* 9 7 8 1 6 4 1 3 3 6 2 8 4 *